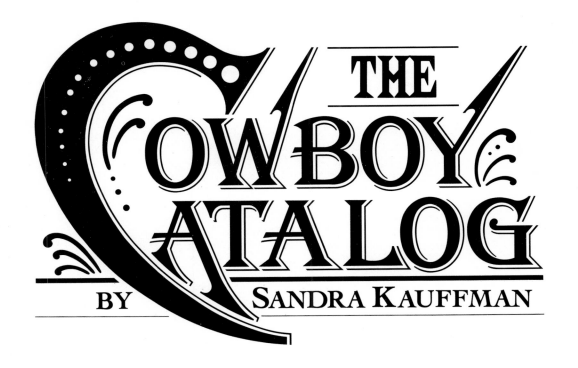

THE COWBOY CATALOG

BY SANDRA KAUFFMAN

FOREWORD BY BILLY MARTIN

Clarkson N. Potter, Inc./Publishers

DISTRIBUTED BY CROWN PUBLISHERS, INC., NEW YORK

To ALEX, just as I promised

PICTURE CREDITS

AMARILLO ART CENTER 22 left. TED BAFALOUKOS 132 lower left. BALDWIN/WATRISS/WOODFIN CAMP 12—13, 158—59. BYER ROLNICK 104—5 bottom. BARBARA BERSELL 15, 61, 101, 130, 147, 169. WALTER BREDEL 33, 115, 152 upper right, 154—55, 156 upper left. JOEL BRODSKY 126 lower right. DAN BUDNIK/WOODFIN CAMP 106—7. DAVID BURNET/CONTACT CAMP 125, 144. BILLY MARTIN'S WESTERN WEAR 59. JODI COBB/WOODFIN CAMP 84 lower left. CULVER PICTURES 78—79. CUTTER BILL 91., EDWARD GRAZDA 122, 148 top, 161, 173. THOMAS HOPKER/WOODFIN CAMP 46—47, 73. BARRY KIESELSTEIN-CORD 150 left, top. KIMBLE STABLES 36 upper right. MATTHEW KLEIN 37 left, 62 upper left, 63 upper right, 64 left, 76—77 upper left, 120—21 center, 120 lower right, 132 upper left, right. SYDNEY and FRANCES LEWIS COLLECTION 88 lower right. LONG BEACH MUSEUM OF ART 18—19. WALLY MCNAMEE/WOODFIN CAMP 50—51. CHRIS MEAD 9, 170—71, 174—75. WAYNE MILLER 105 top left, top right. MOVIE STAR NEWS 70—71. ARTHUR L. PERRY, JR., INTREPID FARMS 85 lower right. PROFESSIONAL COWBOYS RODEO ASSOCIATION 178—79, 180—81. STEVE SMITH 156 bottom. SMITHSONIAN INSTITUTION 52 upper left, 53 lower right. UPI 58. WESTERN OUTFITTER MAGAZINE 176 right center, COLORADO HISTORICAL SOCIETY 113. BARON WOLMAN/WOODFIN CAMP 84 upper left. ADAM WOOLFITT/WOODFIN CAMP 98. WRANGLER 49, 189.

Inquiries should be addressed to Clarkson N. Potter, Inc., One Park Avenue, New York, New York 10016

Printed in Japan by Toppan Printing

Published simultaneously in Canada by General Publishing Company Limited

Library of Congress Cataloging in Publication Data

Kauffman, Sandra.
   The cowboy catalog.
   Includes index.
   1. Rodeos — United States — Equipment and supplies — Catalogs. 2. Cowboys — United States — Costume — Catalogs. 3. Rodeos — United States — Miscellanea. 4. Cowboys — United States — Miscellanea.
   I. Title.
GV1843.3.K38 1980   688.7'8   79-23701
ISBN: 0-517-539500 (cloth)
        0-517-540355 (paper)

10 9 8 7 6 5 4 3 2

CONTENTS

ACKNOWLEDGMENTS

The great Western writer J. Frank Dobie said, "All of us live in debt to each other." While compiling this book, I amassed a number of extraordinary creditors and it is a pleasure to repay them here.
My thanks:

To MARGERY PETERS, the designer of *The Cowboy Catalog,* whose qualities of mind and heart are as exceptional as her talent.

To BERNARD KAUFFMAN, of H. Kauffman & Sons, whose family has been outfitting cowboys for over a century, and whose knowledge of Western saddlery and clothing was invaluable.

To ARTHUR BERWICK, actor, cook, Longview expatriate, and friend, who planned the Texas barbecue, came up with the right word (and ingredient) at the right time, and answered an unconscionable number of questions with unfailing graciousness and tact.

To RICHARD ZEIF, who unearthed a mine of useful information and whose interest in this project and longtime love of the West were a constant delight.

To RAYMOND CORDER, of Blue Bell, Inc., who was one of the first to offer photographs, diagrams, and information, as well as enthusiasm and support.

To DOUG DAHL, of *Tack 'n Togs* magazine, who not only knows "who's who" but "who's where" and put me in touch with so many hard-to-find people.

To JERRY RIDDLE of Cutter Bill Western World, PHILIP LIVINGSTON of Ryon Saddlery, and PATRICK HOULIHAN of Sheplers for their incredible generosity and cooperation.

To photographers WALTER BREDEL, MATTHEW KLEIN, WAYNE MILLER, and JOEL BRODSKY for contributing their talent. And to VALERIE BRODSKY for volunteering Joel.

To E. O. KIMBALL, HELEN CROMBIE, and BETTY REDSTONE, of Kimball's Stables, who provided saddles, books, photographs, tea and sympathy, and a roof over our heads.

To silver experts SHERRON EVINS and R. D. MAGERS, of Diablo, who taught me how to care for Western sterling.

To JOHN R. BOGARDUS of The Driskill, HANS JOHN of The Shamrock Hilton, ART ABBOT of The Menger, and NINFA LAURENZO of Ninfa's, whose superlative recipes appear in the Cowboy Cookbook.

To KENT SMITH, of the Long Beach Museum of Art, and THOMAS A. LIVESAY, of the Amarillo Art Center, for the photographs of Cosimo Lucchese's State Boots. And to the Smithsonian Institution for the photographs of Levi Strauss jeans.

To DAVID ALLEN and KAREN MORRISON of the Professional Rodeo Cowboys Association and to the Girls Rodeo Association for photographs, information, and advice.

To the manufacturers, retailers, and advertising agencies whose generosity and goodwill made this book possible: to CHET VOGT and CARMELLA PERACCA of Vogt Western Silver; WILLIAM M. MANNING and CLIFF LONG of Tex Tan Western Leather Co.; ENID JUSTIN and DALE GORDON of Nocona Boots; SAM LUCCHESE and TONY LAMA, JR., of Tony Lama Co.; JOE EDMONSON and TOM DUFFY of Acme Boots; WILLIAM TILLOU of Lucchese Boots; BOB BLACKWOOD of Bob Blackwood Spurs and Rodeo Equipment; TOM TAYLOR of Tom Taylor Co.; MARVIN J. DOHERTY of Renalde, Crockett & Kelly; ROBERT CRATES, JR., of Simco Leather Co.; JOHN SECREST of the Stetson Hat Co.; CHAR B. DE VAZQUEZ of Char Designs; PHYLLIS TRASK of Austin-Hall Boot Co.; BILL POWERS of The Justin Companies; BOB and ELLA MARCY of Rogue Leather Co.; EDYTHE and NOEL COHEN of Rodeo Shop of Fort Worth; MARY ANN EASLEY of Levi Strauss & Co.; DOUG NEWTON and LARRY DE GRAY of Billy Martin's Western Wear; JOHN MILANO of Byer-Rolnick; BARRY KIESELSTEIN-CORD of Barry Kieselstein Enterprises; DENNIS HIGH of Gerry Western; IRVING SCHOTT, MILTON PERLMAN, and JACK COYNE of Schott Bros.; DANIEL SCULLY and ANN JAMES of Scully Leatherwear; GARNETT FRYE of Trego's Westwear; MARTY ALLEN of Warner's Tack Manufacturing Corp.; H. KEITH NIX of Neiman-Marcus; MIKE HENRY of Nocona Belts; RUDY WEEKS of John A. Frye Shoe Co.; LEO F. LEROY of Durango Boots; WANDA BROWN of Bar W; SY SPINNER of Texas Boots; CHARLES BAILEY of Bailey Hat Co.; STEVE SUSONG of Altman Western Leathers; PAUL CHRISTENFELD of Halpern & Christenfeld; SEYMOUR CHRISTENFELD of California Ranchwear; SAMUEL and CAROL PIERCE of Hartman Trailer; SAM SINKIN of Lasso Western Wear; VIOLET MOSHER of Johnston Trailers; ANN-MARIE GERASIMCHIK of Oleg Cassini; ROBERT PERSONS and PATRICIA NIVER PERSONS of Niver Western Wear; CHARLES YOUNT and BILL TYRRELL of Cherokee Manufacturing Co.; BOB EISENMAN of General Trailer; PRICE McLAUCHLIN of Price McLauchlin Saddle Shop; LEO and SHARON CAMARILLO of Camarillo Enterprises; ANTON J. STARY of Circle Y, Inc.; GAYLIA HALL of Dickson-Jenkins; DON HANDLER and PHILIP B. CLANCY of Champion Western Wear; SONNY HANDLER of Handler-Fenton; P. R. VAN SCOYK of Colorado Saddlery; MARVIN DEBBER of Miller Western Wear; LARRY LYTHGOE and MIKE SHAW of Karman Western Apparel; EDWIN GLICK of The Prior Company; JOHN SULLIVAN and SALLIE HOYT of After Six Formals; TOM KLINGNER of H. D. Lee Co.; DONALD FUTRELL and NANCY NELSON of Raven Industries; NUDIE; PATTY WEINBRENNER of Ackerman & McQueen; GLORIA GIBSON of Admar; SCOTT DALLY and LARRY ROQUEMORE of Dally Advertising; FRANCES WILLIAMS of the Roy Rogers— Dale Evans Museum; CHIP TALBOT of the Men's Fashion Association of America; Country Britches; Condor; DAN TAYLOR of Buccaneer Sportswear; SHELDON KAPLAN of KM & Associates; STAFFORD WERNER of DeBruyn-Rettig; CINDY MURPHY of Wallace Advertising; Above The Crowd; Van Heusen Co.; Mahopa; WARREN SMITH of Chrysler Corporation; ALISON STOOKER of The Ford Motor Co.; General Motors Corporation; International Harvester Co., American Motors Corp.; Sedgefield Sportswear Co.; Sasson Jeans; Le Poché; Salaminder; Sheik Jeans; State of Texas Jeans; JOHN REHEIS of Johnston & Murphy; DAVID BROWDA of Browda Leathers; ED CALVERT of Washington Manufacturing Co.; W. G. POTTS of Potts Longhorn Leather; MORRIS WEINBERG of Prestige West; SYDNEY LONDON of American Feather Co.; VICKY and LARRY WICKEY of The Gift Barn; JOHN CHAMBERS of Chambers Belt Co.; GLEN TAYLOR of Double R Leather Co.; JOANNA TRUEDSSON of Gil Truedsson; HOWARD STEGMAN of Comstock Silversmiths; KEN GRAY of Brookfield; TAD MIZWA of Western Outfitter Magazine; MARY SANDERS of Western Publications, Inc.; Cartier, Inc.; D&D Communications.

To my publisher, JANE WEST, for her faith and enthusiasm, and for many kindnesses; to my editors NANCY NOVOGROD, MICHAEL FRAGNITO, and PAM POLLACK for their care and dedication; to photo researcher JAN TABORELLI; librarian JOAN HEILBRONER of the Town School; FLORENCE STONE of the Museum of Natural History in New York; and typist and baby-sitter par excellence WENDY OHRBACH, for their helpfulness. And to MAXINE NELSON and GLORIA ZEIF for just being there.

Finally, to all the riders of the Kauffman range — my daughters ALEXANDRA and NICOLE, who were patient and understanding; my mother, CELIA BRESLERMAN, who kept our stomachs filled and our spirits high; and, most of all, to CHUCK, who held my hand and made it all come true.

FOREWORD

Western Wear. There's something about it that persists. Somewhere between the rugged reality of a westward-expanding America of one hundred years ago and the automated, controlled, and regulated world of today's corporate existence it endured. It's with us now.

What does Western Wear mean to me? Freedom, comfort, individuality, romance, unlimited possibilities, unlimited horizons; Western Wear is America and American.

I think Western Wear got to me because I spent the greater part of my life in a uniform. Not the gray flannel one of Madison Avenue or the banker's pinstripes. But a baseball uniform I was fiercely proud of and which I worked my tail off in order to wear.

After a game, I'll be damned if I'm gonna trade my baseball uniform for someone else's idea of how an individual should dress. A Yankee pinstripe for a banker's pinstripe? No way.

On the field or off, I felt the need to express part of me, my independence, my self. That's how I got into Western Wear and I haven't been out of it since. And here's the book that will tell *you* all about it.

—BILLY MARTIN
January 15, 1980

INTRODUCTION

The cowboy was a generous and practical hero. Unlike Robin Hood and King Arthur, who rode off into history leaving only their songs and stories behind them, the legendary horseman left us tangible proof of his existence: his clothes and his equipment. What's more, these legacies are not museum pieces but bold and beautiful objects that are as wearable and useful today as they were hundreds of years ago. *Hundreds* of years ago? Yes, for the story of the cowboy and the story of his clothes and equipment really begins in Mexico in 1519, the year Hernando Cortez, the Spanish conquistador, laid siege to the rich Aztec Indian empire. Though Cortez did not have a particularly large army, he managed to subdue thousands of Aztecs and conquer almost all of central and southern Mexico. His secret weapon? The horse. Horses had not lived in North America since the Ice Age, and when Cortez appeared on his magnificent Arabian mount he was thought to be a god.

The Spanish occupation of Mexico lasted for three centuries, and during this period of colonization and change, the seeds of the Western cowboy culture were sown. The Spanish colonists introduced horses and cattle to the New World; then they taught their Indian slaves to ride and put them in charge of their burgeoning herds. These slaves were called "vaqueros," or cowboys (from *vaca*, the Spanish word for "cow"), and by the middle of the eighteenth century they had not only become expert horsemen, but had acquired all the elaborate trappings — the chaps, boots, spurs, sombreros, and saddles — of their Spanish masters.

Eventually, as the cattle industry thrived and the Spanish influence spread northward, the colonists gathered together their slaves and their livestock, crossed the Rio Grande, and put down stakes in what is now Texas and California. In the years that followed, great numbers of horses and cows strayed from the herds, ran wild in the brush, and started to breed and multiply. By 1800 the southwestern deserts were teeming with mustangs and longhorns, and these animals were available — free — to any man who could capture them. Buffalo hunters, Indian scouts, and farmers then went into the cattle business. In 1821, when Mexico won her freedom, she offered large parcels of grazing land to American families who would settle the region east of the Rio Grande. In 1822 there were 150 of these settlers in Texas. By 1836 there were 35,000, and no longer willing to live under Mexican law, they fought for and won their independence.

These first Texans — these hunters and farmers and scouts whose lives revolved around horses and cattle, whose land was a vast, unchartered wilderness — were

A COWBOY takes time off from his daily rounds so his horse can relax, cool down, and graze.

the American cowboy's forebears. And just as they had inherited the Mexican's land and cattle and lifestyle, so too did they inherit his clothes and equipment: the chaps that protected his legs from the brush; the boots that enabled him to grasp the stirrup of his outsized saddle; the wide-brimmed hat that sheltered him from the elements; the bits, bridles, and spurs that allowed him to control his headstrong horses. They even inherited his language. "Buckaroo," one of the synonyms for "cowboy," comes from *vaquero* (the Spanish "v" is pronounced "b"); the lariat was once *la reata*; the hackamore once *jáquima*. Later, of course, this inheritance was modified and transformed as the cowboy struck out on new trails and left his brand on all that he touched.

Cowboys, as we know them, came into existence just after the Civil War. For the most part, they were Texans and former Confederate soldiers who came West to seek their fortunes in the booming stock industry. When the war ended, they saw the price of beef skyrocket, and knew that cattle could be sold in the East for great profit. They also knew that in order to be shipped East, the cattle had to be driven to railroad towns hundreds of miles away. For thirty dollars a month, these veterans agreed to a life of danger, hardship, and loneliness, and set off on a trail that started in Texas and eventually led through the Great Plains, the Great Basin, and the Rocky Mountains, as far north as Canada and as far west as California, Idaho, and Utah.

By 1895 the adventure was over. The railroads had grown, the trails had closed, cattle raising had become a business like any other. But when the drama ended, the legend began, and the best part of that legend — the truest part — lives on in the cowboy's extraordinary clothes and equipment.

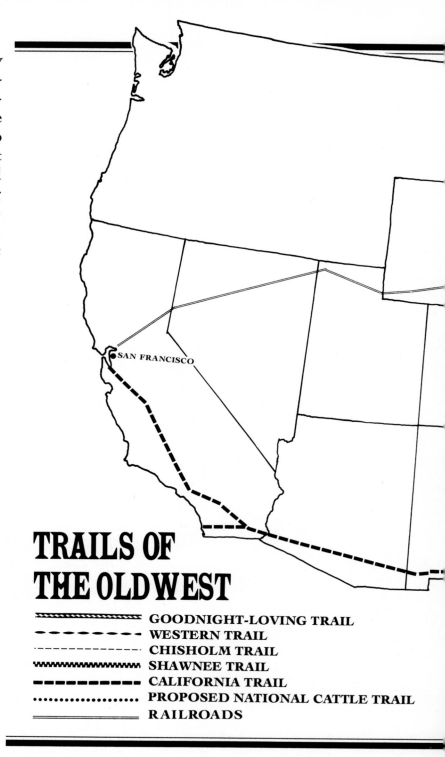

TRAILS OF THE OLD WEST

〰〰〰〰	GOODNIGHT-LOVING TRAIL
– – – –	WESTERN TRAIL
- - - - -	CHISHOLM TRAIL
wwwwwwww	SHAWNEE TRAIL
▬ ▬ ▬ ▬	CALIFORNIA TRAIL
••••••••	PROPOSED NATIONAL CATTLE TRAIL
═══════	RAILROADS

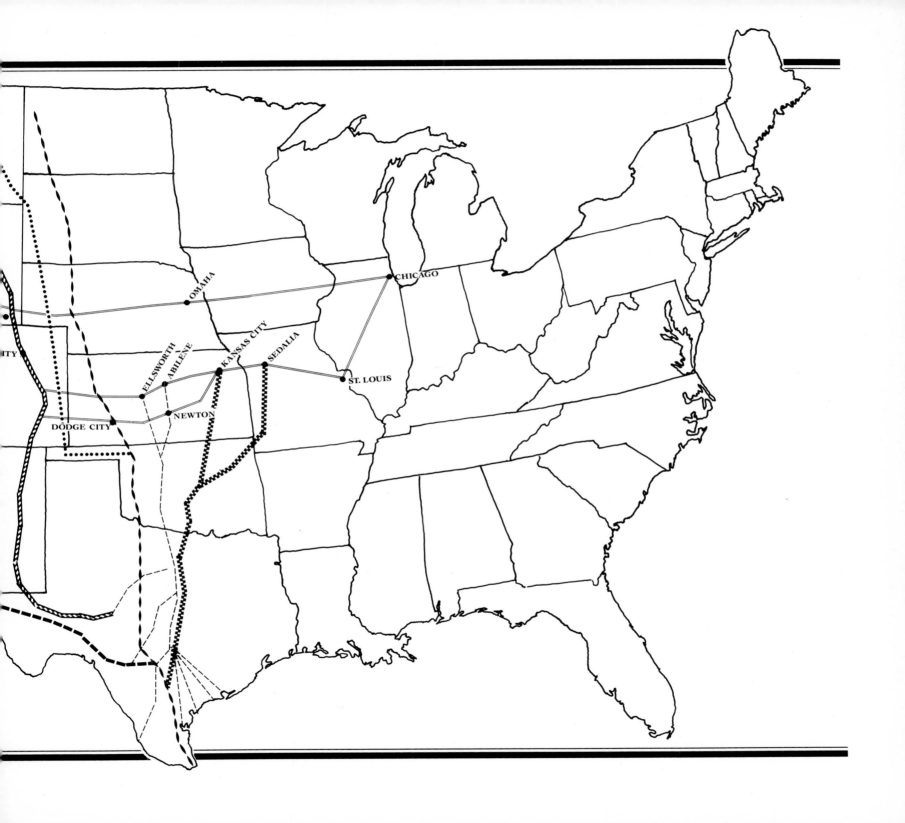

BOOTS

We used to make them to fit a stirrup. Now we make them to fit the gas pedal of a Cadillac."

The speaker was the late Cosimo Lucchese, master bootmaker, and in two sentences he told not only the story of the Western boot, but the story of the West itself.

Like the men who wore them and the country that bred them, Western boots have grown richer, grander, and more dazzling with the years. Looking at the intricate designs, brilliant colors, and exotic skins of today, an oldtime cowboy would melt with envy.

In his day, a boot was not a luxury or a thing of beauty but a necessary tool of the trade. It was a piece of equipment, like a knife or a lariat, and it was worn for protection, not adornment. For the man who roped steers and broke horses, whose work demanded consummate balance and a sturdy grip, the correct boot could mean the difference between life and death, and there was only one correct boot. Made of horsehide or muleskin, it was as ugly as homemade soap but it was a masterpiece of design.

The boot had a narrow toe that could find the stirrup quickly when a horse acted up, and it was loose on top, so it could be kicked off in a hurry if the cowboy got hung-up (see Texas Talk, page 122) or entangled.

Knee-high, with long, mule-ear pull straps, it was a shield against stones and rubble, against the thorns of the mesquite tree, against cow paddies and snakes. It kept the stirrups from bruising the cowboy's ankles, and the stirrup leathers from rubbing his legs. Best of all, it had a high, underslung heel that helped the cowboy in a thousand ways. That heel burrowed into the earth and braced him when he wrestled bulls or led his horse down a steep hill. It kept his foot from slipping through the thick wooden stirrup of the Western saddle, so that if he were thrown, he would not be trapped in that stirrup and dragged along the ground.

Still, even the Western boot had its shortcomings. One of these sounded loud and clear at dances and town meetings: the darn thing squeaked! Of course, there was a remedy — soaking the boots in water helped — but quiet conversation was always an uphill battle. To make matters worse, that two-inch heel was murder to walk on. If the cowboy had to make it home on foot, he took off his boots. They were designed, he said, by scheming horse dealers, to make sure he never left the saddle.

We do not know who actually designed the Western boot. We *do* know that it was a direct outgrowth of the cowboy's needs, of his life, of his work and his environment. In the early days of the West, he had gone

HIGH HEELS, elaborate stitching, and fanciful designs have made the American cowboy boot famous throughout the world.

up the Chisholm Trail in shoes, or, if he was lucky, in an old pair of Confederate cavalry boots. His need for good footwear eventually brought European boot-makers to the West. These craftsmen took the Spanish riding boot that the Conquistadors had brought to Mexico and transformed it into something truly American.

They stitched the top of the boot to keep it from buckling and chafing the cowboy's leg, and soon their black and brown threads burst into color, and their simple stitch patterns blossomed into stars and swirls and eagles' wings.

They made a square, narrow toe to fit the tapadero (stirrup cover) of the Spanish saddle, and eventually that toe grew long and sharp enough to spear a coyote.

Later, as chaps gained in popularity, boots became shorter; the old stovepipe top disappeared, replaced by a shapely scalloped edge. As the cowboy pros-pered, the leather on his boots grew finer, softer, and more exotic, and, when the jeep finally replaced the horse, the high, underslung heel — the soul of the old Western boot — began to shrink. Once the cowboy found himself on the ground — fixing flat tires and walking to the station when the jeep ran out of gas — the 2-inch heel became a 1¾-inch heel and that, in turn, became a 1¼-inch heel. The old boot was dead.

However, like all good Westerns, this, too, has a happy ending: As the space-age cowboy rides off into the sunset, his dual-wheeled pickup hugging the superhighway, that boot on his foot looks vaguely fa-miliar. Knee-high, with pull straps and a short, narrow toe, it actually has a two-inch high, underslung heel!

What's going on? "The real trend today is back to the Old West look," says *Western Outfitter. Tack 'n Togs* magazine agrees: "Everyone wants that old cowboy image."

The good guys always win.

THE ORIGINAL Frye boot. Designed in 1863, Frye's tough, square-toed work boot has be-come an American classic and is avail-able today in tan, rust, black, and antique brown cow-hide. $85.

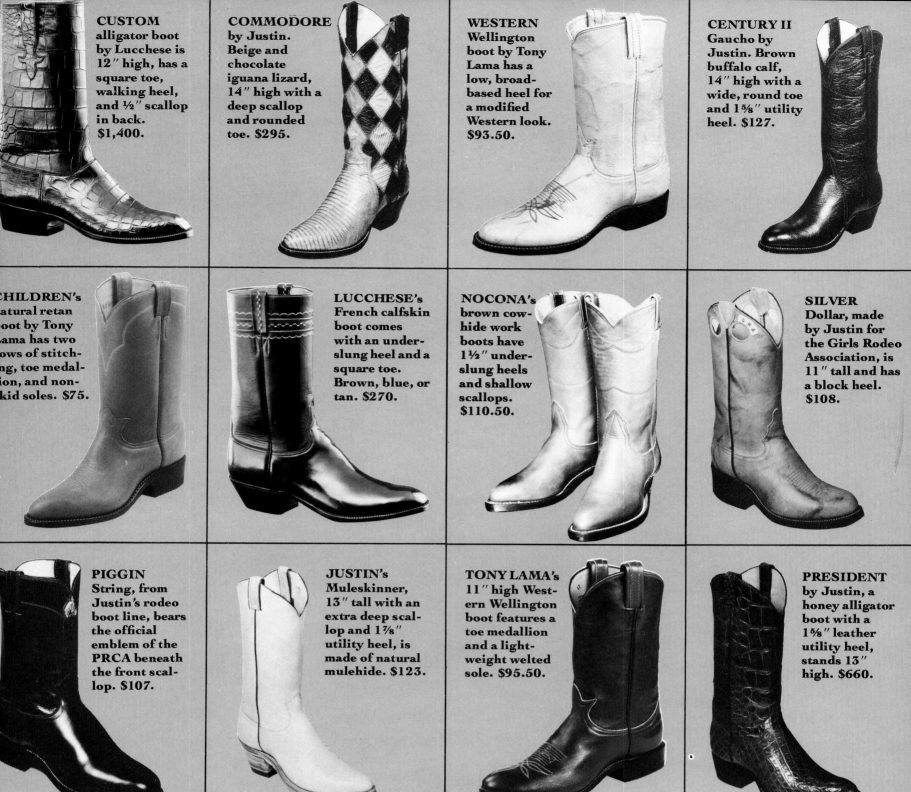

CUSTOM alligator boot by Lucchese is 12″ high, has a square toe, walking heel, and ½″ scallop in back. $1,400.

COMMODORE by Justin. Beige and chocolate iguana lizard, 14″ high with a deep scallop and rounded toe. $295.

WESTERN Wellington boot by Tony Lama has a low, broad-based heel for a modified Western look. $93.50.

CENTURY II Gaucho by Justin. Brown buffalo calf, 14″ high with a wide, round toe and 1⅝″ utility heel. $127.

CHILDREN's natural retan boot by Tony Lama has two rows of stitching, toe medallion, and non-skid soles. $75.

LUCCHESE's French calfskin boot comes with an under-slung heel and a square toe. Brown, blue, or tan. $270.

NOCONA's brown cowhide work boots have 1½″ under-slung heels and shallow scallops. $110.50.

SILVER Dollar, made by Justin for the Girls Rodeo Association, is 11″ tall and has a block heel. $108.

PIGGIN String, from Justin's rodeo boot line, bears the official emblem of the PRCA beneath the front scallop. $107.

JUSTIN's Muleskinner, 13″ tall with an extra deep scallop and 1⅞″ utility heel, is made of natural mulehide. $123.

TONY LAMA's 11″ high Western Wellington boot features a toe medallion and a lightweight welted sole. $95.50.

PRESIDENT by Justin, a honey alligator boot with a 1⅝″ leather utility heel, stands 13″ high. $660.

WHAT TO LOOK FOR IN A WESTERN BOOT

A Good Boot Should Have:

A STEEL SHANK Wood will not give you enough arch support. Most of the better boots are made with steel, but if you are not sure of what you are getting, ask your salesman.

A PEGGED SHANK Another must for proper arch support. Make sure the pegs are set close together and that there are plenty of them or the steel shank will wear right through the sole. Wooden pegs are best, but since they expand in warm weather and contract in cold, they are usually reinforced with brass nails.

A LEATHER LINING Man-made fabrics are not very compatible with leather. They do not expand and contract at the same rate as leather and will eventually separate from the boot and tear.

SMOOTH MESHING of HEEL and TOE If there is a gap at the point where they join — beware! The heel may loosen and fall off.

SOLID WORKMANSHIP You can tell a lot about a boot by the way it is stitched and sewn. If the quality is poor, the stitching on the face and on the outer sole will be uneven, the stitching on the insole will stand up, and the pull straps will be loose or asymmetrical.

A Riding Boot Should Have:

AN UNDERSLUNG HEEL This gives you a good grip on the stirrup and keeps your foot from sliding through it.

A TAPERED TOE This helps you find your stirrup easily. Tapered does not mean needle-sharp or even pointed, but it does mean that the toe is fairly narrow rather than wide and blunt.

A HARD SOLE This keeps nails, rocks, and other debris from penetrating your feet. The synthetics — neoprene and neolite — are your best bets. Rubber is shorter-lived, and though leather is fine on solid ground, it tends to be slippery on floors and pavement. Spongy materials, such as Vibram and crepe, cling to the stirrups and should be avoided. *Caution:* When your boots need resoling, the entire sole must be taken off and replaced. Half-soles are very dangerous on riding boots — they curl up and catch in the stirrups.

A MINIMUM OF DECORATION Be as bold as you like with pattern and color but steer clear of rings, straps, buckles, bangles, and other fancy trimmings that catch on equipment and cause accidents.

The Boot Should Fit the Foot

Cowboy boots are not only great to look at, they're incredibly comfortable. Doubt it? One good fit will make a believer of you. Here's how to get it. (With a little help from Tony Lama.)

INSTEP Because it has no laces, straps, or zippers to bind it to the foot, a Western boot will not be secure unless it fits snugly in the instep. Often, you can estimate the tightness or looseness of the instep by the width of the throat. If your foot slips into the throat too easily, chances are the instep is too loose and you need a narrower boot.

BALL The ball of your foot must always rest on the ball (the widest part) of the last. If it sits too far forward (as it will if you wear too short a boot), your toes will be crammed into the toe box and will develop corns from rubbing against the inner lining of the boot. What's more, your toes will hang over the welt, push the boot out of shape, and shorten its life.

HEEL Don't expect the heel of a Western boot to hug your foot when you walk — it

20

will always slip a bit. This slippage may be quite pronounced when the boot is new and the sole is stiff and unyielding, but after several wearings, the sole will begin to flex, and most of the slippage will disappear.

If you try on a boot that has no slippage whatsoever, it is either too short for you or too tight in the instep, and

will raise blisters on your heel. If you try on one that slips excessively, it is too loose in the instep and you need a narrower width — not a shorter boot!

A boot with a properly fitted heel will always be a little hard to pull on and off. A silicone spray (It and Hush are good), applied above the heel area, will ease the way with-

out damaging the leather. And remember: Don't try to pull on a boot from a sitting position; stand up and step down into it, and you will not have to work quite so hard.

HEIGHT The height of your heel always affects the fit of your boot, and you will find that a high-heeled (two

inches or over) boot can be worn narrower and shorter than a low-heeled one. Because a high-heeled boot concentrates your weight on the ball of your foot and keeps that foot fairly rigid, your toes need very little room to flex. However, when you wear a low-heeled boot, your weight is distributed over your entire arch area, and your foot flattens out. You then need extra length and width to accommodate your spreading toes.

TOES Your toes are in the right position if they touch, *but do not push against* the inner wall of your boot when you stand.

LENGTH AND WIDTH "Of all the fitting sins, the short fit is the most harmful and the most common. The longer your fit," says Sam Lucchese, "the better off you are. A longer, narrower fit will overcome pressure on the big toe and give you more support in the arch and the all-important metatarsal area."

IN GENERAL A properly fitted boot does not require a breaking-in period. If your boot does not feel good the moment you put it on, it isn't right for you.

PARTS OF THE BOOT

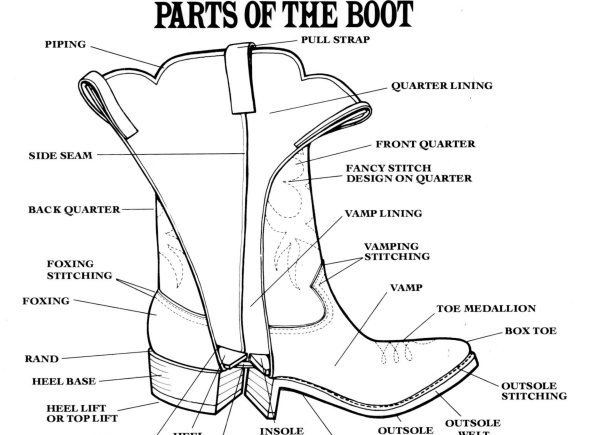

PIPING

PULL STRAP

QUARTER LINING

FRONT QUARTER

FANCY STITCH
DESIGN ON QUARTER

SIDE SEAM

VAMP LINING

BACK QUARTER

VAMPING
STITCHING

VAMP

FOXING
STITCHING

TOE MEDALLION

FOXING

BOX TOE

RAND

OUTSOLE
STITCHING

HEEL BASE

HEEL LIFT
OR TOP LIFT

OUTSOLE
WELT

COUNTER   HEEL   INSOLE   OUTSOLE
PAD   SHANK   SHANK PEGS

INLAYS & OVERLAYS

Bootmakers achieve their most elaborate effects through the use of inlays and overlays. An inlay is a piece of exotic or colorful leather that is cut into a special shape (i.e., a star, map, or flower) and set *into* the surface of the boot. An overlay is also a decorative piece of leather, but one that is placed *on top of* the boot's surface.

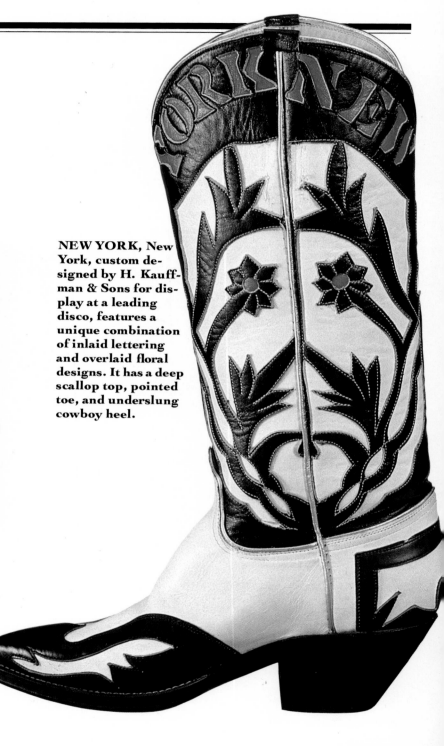

NEW YORK, New York, custom designed by H. Kauffman & Sons for display at a leading disco, features a unique combination of inlaid lettering and overlaid floral designs. It has a deep scallop top, pointed toe, and underslung cowboy heel.

THIS STATE of Texas boot, complete with lone star, mockingbird, and longhorn, was part of a special project begun in the 1940s by master craftsman Cosimo Lucchese. The son of an Italian immigrant, Lucchese wanted to honor each of the forty-eight states with an original pair of boots depicting its flag, bird, animal, flower, and Capitol building. Eventually, forty-two pairs of highly colorful, intricately inlaid, and overlaid boots were completed and, in 1976, they were sent on a bicentennial tour of the nation's museums by Acme Boots, their present owner. Further examples of state boots can be seen on pages 18 and 19.

EXTRA-DEEP scallop makes Justin's Lady Sundown easy to pull on. $156.

FLYING Eagle combines inlays and overlays. Austin-Hall for H. Kauffman & Sons. $250.

DAISY by Justin is 15″ tall, has a deep scallop, and 1⅞″ underslung heel. $168.

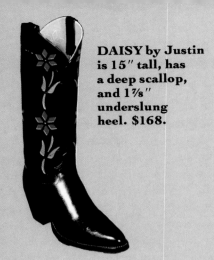

JUSTIN Signature Edition, signed by John Justin and inlaid with the map of Texas. $600.

...ACHE Flower has overlaid toe ... heel caps. Austin-Hall for ... Kauffman & Sons. $275.

ACME's Appalachian features a medium narrow toe, a beige lizard foot, and a bone shaft. $173.

CUSTOM boot, made by Nocona for singer Jerry Jeff Walker, has ostrich vamp, inlaid shaft.

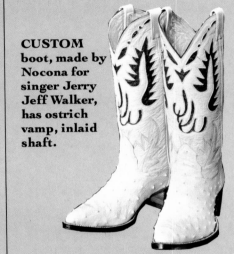

INLAID butterflies are set off by a double row of stitching on Justin's 17″ ladies' boot. $189.

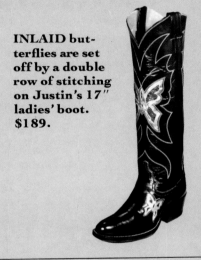

...N insets and
...tching on
...ck patent
...ther high-
...ht Acme's
...ssissippi
...mbler. $79.

INTRICATE cutouts and overlays define the Yankee Special by H. Kauffman & Sons. $350.

MARSHAL, from Justin's one-hundredth anniversary collection, is 13″ high, deeply scalloped. $156.

POWDER River has matching collar and inlays. Austin-Hall for H. Kauffman & Sons. $265.

HEEL STYLES

When Genghis Khan and his Mongol hordes came galloping out of Asia in the thirteenth century, they left their mark on Western feet as well as on Western consciousness. Because they were professional horsemen, they wore boots with high, wooden heels, and because horses were such luxuries, those heels came to symbolize wealth and power. "Well-heeled" became synonymous with "well-to-do," and the high-heeled boot became a badge of honor, a sign of the knight and the cavalier, men who rode horses and were better than men who walked.

Today, high, underslung heels are so closely identified with cowboy boots that Western aficionados find all other heels objectionable. This makes the rebels mad. They say that high heels are as barbaric as the Great Khan himself, that they are just a bit more comfortable to walk on than hot coals, and that if they have any appeal whatsoever, it falls somewhere between macho and Masoch. Others, more romantic, feel that the heels are dashing and exciting, and would gladly wear them — if they could. But these willing spirits find their flesh (and their arches) all too weak.

Fortunately, modern boots are made with many different types of heels, and purists and rebels need not shoot it out at the local bootery. A little frontier tolerance, and both will find exactly what they're looking for.

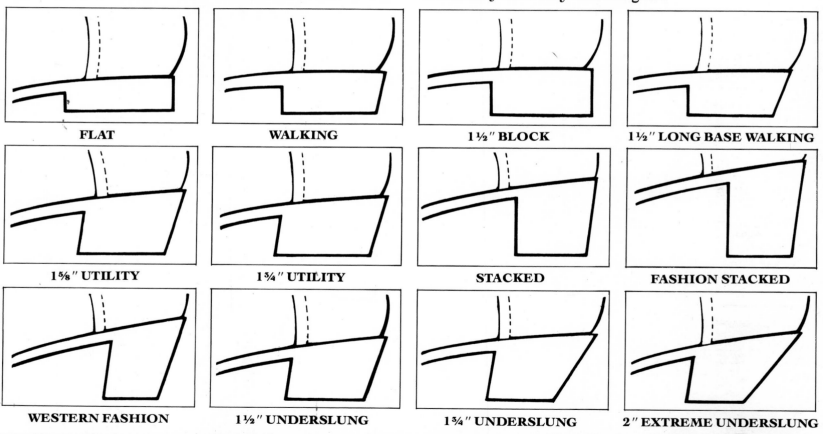

FLAT	WALKING	1½″ BLOCK	1½″ LONG BASE WALKING
1⅝″ UTILITY	1¾″ UTILITY	STACKED	FASHION STACKED
WESTERN FASHION	1½″ UNDERSLUNG	1¾″ UNDERSLUNG	2″ EXTREME UNDERSLUNG

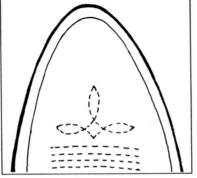
NARROW POINTED

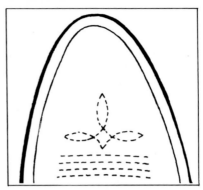
WELLINGTON

MEDIUM ROUND

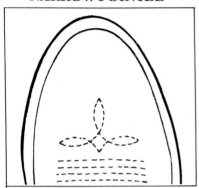
ROUND

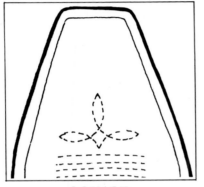
SQUARE

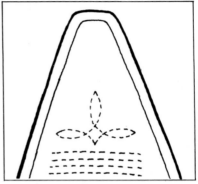
NARROW SQUARE

TOE STYLES

Think of cowboy boots and you think of long, needle-sharp toes that resemble the horns of a Texas steer. Truth to tell, the needle toe did not come into fashion until after World War II and, aside from being completely useless (one supporter did say it was good for squashing bugs in corners), was notable only for getting itself scraped and stepped on. Today, the original square toe and the gently rounded toe are back, but there are still some pointy hangers-on. Sam Lucchese explains why: "Toe styles are slow to grow and slow to go. The entire older generation has to be gone completely before a toe style fades. Because it was 'their' toe, they aren't about to give it up and will die wearing it."

And how do new styles get started? "Every kid, as soon as he is old enough to buy his own boots, has to buy something different from what his daddy wore. So, about every generation, bootmakers come up with a new toe."

Toe Wrinkles, or Medallions Medallions allow the toes to crease along natural lines and prevent unsightly ridges from developing on the surface of the boot.

TOP CUTS

Scallops and pull-straps make today's tall boots easier to get into.

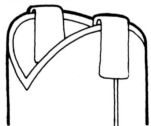
STOVEPIPE TOP

SHALLOW SCALLOP

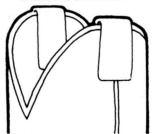
DEEP SCALLOP

EXTRA DEEP SCALLOP

25

STITCHING

Looking at the colorful threads swirling up and down and around today's boots, it is hard to believe that stitching once had (and, to a lesser degree, still has) a specific purpose. In fact, it was the early bootmaker's answer to a very real problem: How to make a tall boot stand up straight and retain its shape.

Because the old Spanish boot was made from two pieces of leather and wet-boned (shaped while the leather was wet), it could be stomped on by a herd of buffalo without losing its lovely lines. The Western boot with its four-piece construction and cheaper method of shaping keeled over and chafed the cowboy's leg. Fortunately, its inventors were a tenacious lot, and refused to accept defeat. A row of stitching in the right place soon proved a double blessing: It not only held up the boot, it held the eye. Before long,

everyone said that "if one row is good, two will be even better," and, today, a boot with eight rows of stitching is not considered unusual. (According to Cosimo Lucchese: one to three rows of stitching—good for a work boot; four rows—okay for a dress boot, but a little short; six rows—real class, gives body to the design; eight rows—too fancy; Hollywood boots!)

Despite all the elaboration, today's stitch patterns are basically the same ones that graced the early boots. Like cattle brands, they were designed originally for specific people. A rancher, for example, would have a pattern made for him, wear it on all his boots, and pass it along to his children. Others adopted (swiped) it, and since manufacturers know a good thing when they see it, the pattern you pick for the discotheque may have once danced at the Lone Star Cafe.

MADE-TO-MEASURE in brown, rust, bone, or black, the horn-back lizard Aristocrat has a 12″ calfskin upper and seven rows of colorful stitching. A scalloped overlay sets off its medium round toe. Ryon Saddlery. $565.

WRANGLER's deeply scalloped, two-tone boots are enhanced by elaborate stitchery. $70.

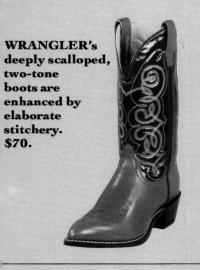

TONY LAMA's Black Toro has four rows of red and white stitching plus red piping on the side and scallop. $124.

JUNGLE KING by Justin, 14″ high with a black and white python vamp and collar, stitched coffee shaft. $210.

POINTY stitchery on Acme's Success echoes the design of the boot's genuine lizard wing tip. $90.

HIGHLY burnished Texas boot has birds of paradise stitched on its front and back. $90.

NOCONA's dress boot features a stitched kid top and buffalo calf vamp. $125.

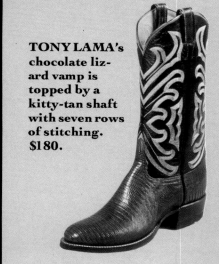

TONY LAMA's chocolate lizard vamp is topped by a kitty-tan shaft with seven rows of stitching. $180.

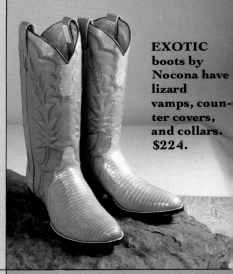

EXOTIC boots by Nocona have lizard vamps, counter covers, and collars. $224.

SWIRLS of multicolored stitching dress up a traditional boot by Nocona. $110.

TONY LAMA's 13″ full scallop boot has a bull-hide vamp and light stitching on a dark shaft. $120.

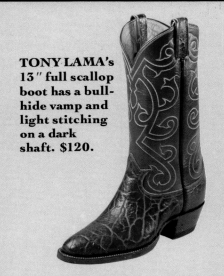

STITCHED Durango boots have ostrich vamps and leather lacings. $175.

STITCHED dress boot by Lucchese features an alligator vamp, matching collar, and pull straps. $788.

THE NAME GAME

Sorting out the big names in the boot world can be baffling but fun! Enid Justin, for example. You might expect to find her on the Board of Directors of the Justin Boot Company. Wrong. When her brothers moved the family business to Fort Worth, the fabulous Miss Enid (now eighty-five years old and still making boots) stayed put in Nocona and founded her own company. (The Nocona Boot Company, what else?) Then there is Sam Lucchese, a name you would immediately associate with the Lucchese Boot Company. No way. Sam is no longer associated with the Lucchese Boot Company. Lucchese Boots is now a division of Blue Bell, and Sam has joined the Tony Lama Company, run by Tony Lama, Jr., and located on Tony Lama Street in El Paso. The Tony Lama Company is not to be confused with Tony Lama Leather Products, Inc., which makes its home on Will Rogers Boulevard in Fort Worth. And don't forget the Larry Mahan Boot Collection on Larry Mahan Drive (El Paso, again). P.S. Looking for the Texas Boot Company? You'll find it in Lebanon, Tennessee.

H. J. JUSTIN *(left foreground)* stands inside his newly equipped boot factory in Nocona, Texas. In 1911, the year this photograph was taken, the average price of boots was $11 a pair.

CARING FOR YOUR BOOTS

Although leather prices have shot up higher than a cat's back, good boots are still a sound investment. If cared for properly, they last for years and pay for themselves many times over.

The first thing to remember is to keep them clean. Wipe them with a dry cloth after every wearing and go over them with saddle soap when they get really dirty. Saddle soap is easy to use; it doesn't need to be rubbed in. Apply it to the leather with a clean, damp sponge or cloth, then wipe off the excess. Be careful when you use it on stitching; if the threads get too wet, they will eventually dry up and crack.

While the boots are still damp from the soap, apply a coat of leather conditioner (Lexol and Goddard's Saddler's Wax are both good) to seal in their natural oils and preserve suppleness. Drying may take as long as twenty-four hours, and the boots will still feel somewhat tacky when they are ready for polishing.

Cream polishes, such as Propert's and Meltonian, are best for leather because they penetrate the skin without clogging the pores. Wax polishes are all right too, provided you use them sparingly and buff them well, but liquids neither penetrate nor protect, and many contain harsh ingredients that can damage the skins.

When caring for your boots, always remember that

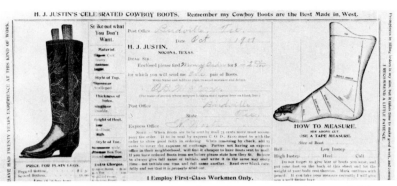

SELF-MEASURING order blank made Justin boots available to cowboys throughout the country and doubled Justin's business.

IN 1948 Justin's daughter, Miss Enid, moved her thriving boot business to larger quarters.

JUSTIN'S BRONC Rider boot was made in the 1920s.

EARLY JUSTIN, circa 1910, with heart-shaped inlay.

---

leather, like all skin, must breathe. Do not saturate it with heavy oils, waxes, or stains, or with any liquid — including water — that will seal its pores and make it harden and crack.

Store your boots in a cool, dry place, away from cold, dampness, and direct sunlight. A clear silicone spray will help protect them from rain and snow, but do not expect leather boots to stand in for rubber ones. Wetness pulls leather out of shape, rots threads, and loosens soles. If you get caught in a storm, allow your boots to dry at room temperature, then apply a leather conditioner. If they are wet inside, stuff them with newspaper to soak up the moisture. *Never* dry your boots in direct heat or place them on a radiator. Heat cracks them and destroys their luster.

If you wear your boots for riding, you should know that the sweat of the horse is apt to discolor them. To minimize the damage, give them the saddle soap treatment after dismounting, then put them on boot trees to air out. Boot trees, incidentally, are a great way to keep your boots in shape and stop the leather from curling. Wooden trees are expensive — about $150 — but an $18 aluminum pair will do the job just as well.

Finally, if you are lucky enough to own more than one pair of boots, alternate them. Do not wear the same pair every day. Variety not only spices up life, it prolongs it.

CUSTOM BOOTS

Anne Baxter wanted multicolored butterflies on hers. LBJ wanted the map of Texas on his. An oilman with a penchant for monograms ordered gold and silver for daytime, diamonds and rubies for evening.

Custom boots pamper your psyche as well as your feet. If you long to tell the world who you are and what you stand for, forget your analyst and find yourself a good custom bootmaker. Lucchese's of San Antonio, for example. In business since 1883, the Luccheses have put everything on footwear except "a picture of someone's mother-in-law." They can immortalize your favorite horse, your prize Brahma, your hometown, or your best girl, and they can do it in 125 different types of leather.

Naturally, such services do not come cheap (prices start at approximately $400), but when you consider that Lucchese is to boots what Neiman-Marcus is to class, it seems downright parsimonious to haggle. Of course, you may blanch a bit when you hear that the expense is not limited to the boots: There is also the plane fare to San Antonio. Like true royalty, the Luccheses do not come to you — you go to them. You go, like Teddy Roosevelt, Tom Mix, Gene Autry, John Wayne, and innumerable Rockefellers have gone before you, to have your feet measured by the masters. And if you think that enshrinement in Grauman's Chinese is the ultimate podiatric experience, wait until you get to Texas.

When you arrive, you will stand on a large, open ledger to have the outlines of your feet traced in pencil. This ritual not only sets you above the crowd, but guarantees you a unique brand of immortality. Luc-

IN 1979, H. Kauffman & Sons asked several well-known American artists to execute paintings on Western boots. The dreamlike landscape with mesas and mythic horses at left is by Paul Brach. The stylized griffin at right, by Finn.

chese's ledgers are filled with outlines of the world's most important feet, and the early volumes are now part of the Barker Texas History Collection in Austin.

When your outlines are completed, measurements are taken of the ball and waist of your foot, of your high instep, your low instep, your heel, and your calf. The results are inscribed in the ledger, like a set of Commandments from Sinai, and you are ready for the pedograph. This is an inked footprint that reveals the pressure points on the sole of your foot, and it is the final step save one: a tracing of your upper foot by an instrument called a contour gauge. All vital statistics in, Lucchese is now ready to construct a wooden last, a replica of your entire foot on which your boot will be built.

In any discussion of boots and bootmaking, one question is inevitable: Does "custom-made" mean "handmade"? The answer is both yes and no. Though

PAUL WHITEMAN, famous in the 1930s and 1940s as the King of Jazz, was an expert Western horseman as well as a fine musician. His beautifully inlaid boots, custom-made by Justin, pay tribute to both his extraordinary talents.

COWBOY STAR Tom Mix, wearing his custom-designed Justins.

STARS, HELMETS, and stitchery enliven Tony Lama's white bullhide boots, designed and manufactured for the Dallas Cowboys football team.

the majority of boots is made mostly by machine, there are still some craftsmen who turn out a completely handmade product. These include James Leddy of Abilene, Tex Robin of Coleman, and Victor Borg of the Stewart Boot Company in Tucson. Lucchese, using both hand and machine, represents a modern-day compromise between the two extremes. Their reasoning? "For some jobs machines have been developed that can and will do a better job than a man can do by hand." Purists may argue the point, but, as they say, "Ya pays yer money and ya takes yer choice."

"Yer choice," however, may depend less on what you want than on where you live. Like Lucchese, most of the custom bootmakers insist that you come in person to be measured, and if you don't happen to live in the southwestern United States, you have a problem. Of course, if you don't want your boots custom fitted, but only custom styled, you have no problem at all.

Practically every boot company will let you choose the skin you want, in the style, color, and design you want, provided you work with a stock last.

When it comes to custom boots, there are only two things you really need: money ("We decide what the price will be after the boots are made" — Lucchese) and patience. For any custom work at all, whether fitting or styling, the minimum wait is approximately seventeen weeks; when you order from top craftsmen like Lucchese, it is more apt to be eighteen months. All of which leads us to the ultimate question: Are custom boots really necessary? The answer is that 80 percent of the boot-buying public can wear a stock last, and unless you have an extremely high instep or an unusual orthopedic problem, you should have no trouble obtaining a good fit from the ready-mades now on the market.

SADDLES

According to Webster, a saddle is a "seat for a rider on the back of a horse." For a cowboy, however, particularly an old-timer, a saddle cannot be defined in cold technical terms. It is not a utilitarian mix of leather and metal, or a tool to subdue an animal. It is his soul. His most precious possession. The symbol of his profession, setting him apart from all other men.

The old-time cowboy paid dearly for his saddle. It was unquestionably the most expensive piece of equipment he owned, and he often joked about its superiority to his mount. "A fifty-dollar saddle on a ten-dollar horse" was the way he put it. But jokes aside, a saddle was a serious matter, and its importance had little to do with its price. The saddle established the cowboy's identity; it was his calling card, a declaration of his status and his financial worth. To part with it would have been unthinkable. To sell it, a disgrace. The Faustian cowboy might play poker with the Devil, might pledge his horse (if he owned one), his gun, his boots, or his brand-new chaps, but never his saddle. His feelings on the subject were so well known that they produced an addition to the language: the expression *he's sold his saddle,* meaning that one (not necessarily a cowboy) has lost all integrity, has relinquished his birthright. To illustrate the point, Philip Ashton Rollins, in his book *The Cowboy,* tells the story of the Montana schoolboy who, when asked who Benedict Arnold was and what he had done, replied: "He was one of our generals, and he sold his saddle."

Although the cowboy, unlike the vaquero, did not make his own saddle, he treated it as if it were born of his own flesh. And, in a way, it was. He rode it for eight to ten hours a day, and by the time it was fully broken in, the contours of its seat were an exact replica of his own. Because he spent so much time in it and because it was such a necessary part of his profession, the cowboy's saddle has often been called his workbench. In reality, it was more than that. It was his spiritual home, the place in which he felt most at ease and the one place to which he could always return. The cowboy was an itinerant worker, a man with no roots and no ties. As soon as he had delivered his herd, he was free to go his own way. Home was wherever he happened to be or wherever a job was waiting. And, wherever that was, there was only one thing he could really count on: the saddle beneath him.

THE SADDLE is the symbol of the cowboy's profession, and in the old trail days it was his most precious possession.

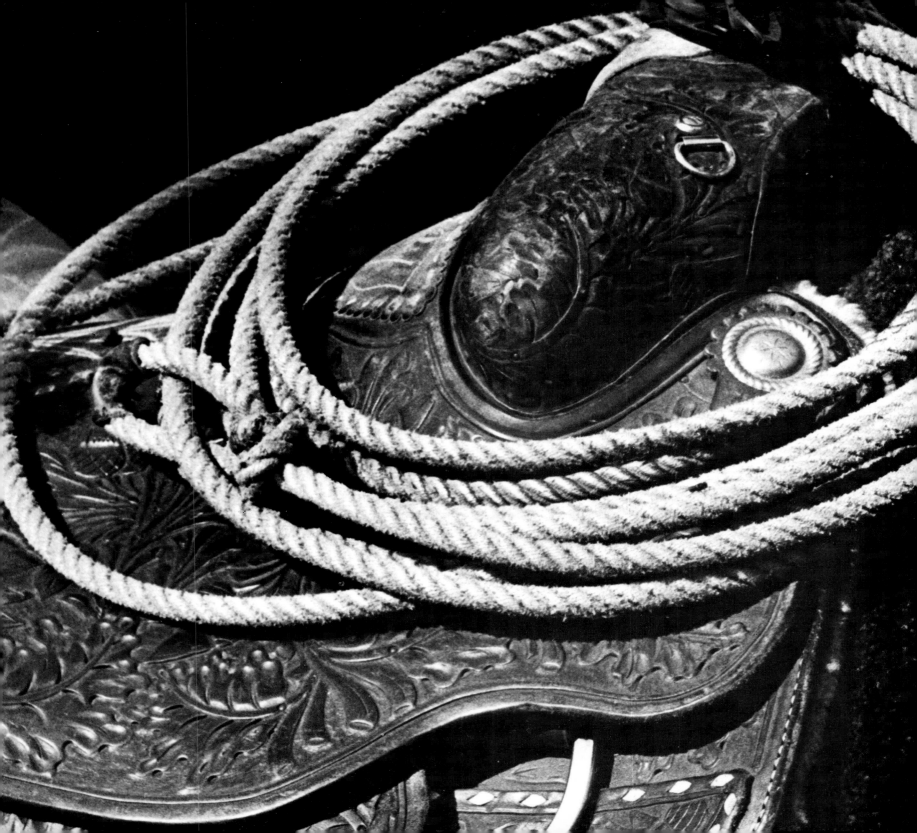

PARTS OF THE SADDLE

The most outstanding feature of the Western saddle is its great size. Unlike its English counterpart, it was built for work, not pleasure, and had to be sturdy enough to support the cowboy as he roped and herded cattle. It also had to be heavy and strong enough to withstand the charge of a raging bull and the crush of working horses.

The saddle weighs between thirty and fifty pounds and is constructed around a wood or fiberglass frame called a *tree*. The tree consists of three main parts: the *cantle*, or backrest; the *fork*, or front, to which the *horn* is later attached; and two side pieces called *bars*, which connect the fork and the cantle, and combine to form the seat. The tree sits low on the horse's back so that the saddle cannot easily be rocked or pulled off, and the deep seat and high cantle assure the cowboy's comfort and stability. The saddle is held in place by the *cincha*, a wide cotton or mohair band that goes under the horse's belly, and by the *latigo*, a long leather strap that is attached at one end to the rigging ring and at the other end to the cincha. A saddle with one cincha is called a *single rig;* a saddle with two cinchas, a *double rig*. Three types of single rigs are the *Spanish rig* (rigging rings located at the front of the saddle), the *center-fire rig* (rings located in the middle of the saddle), and the *three-fourths rig* (rings located three-quarters of the way to the front of the saddle).

The wide, heavy *stirrups* are made of either wood or metal, and keep the cowboy's feet from being scratched by thorns or crushed by trees, cattle, or falling horses. The stirrups are fastened to the tree with straps called *stirrup leathers*, and a leather shield known as a *fender*, or *rosadero*, keeps the leathers from rubbing the horse's sides and the cowboy's legs. The fender is also a protection against the horse's sweat.

The saddle generally has a number of *saddle strings*, or *wang strings*, in front and in back that hold it together and are used to tie on necessary pieces of equipment like slickers, bedrolls, and saddlebags.

The intricate leather carving and stamping that is so much a part of the Western saddle is functional as well as ornamental. It creates friction between rider and saddle and that friction helps to strengthen the rider's seat.

In the old days the *horn* served as an anchor for the cowboy's rope when he roped and branded cattle. A roper was either a tieman or a dallyman. The dallyman used a rawhide riata that was apt to snap under pressure, and so he wrapped, or "dallied," it several times around the horn to make it "give" when the steer pulled at it. The tieman used a hard-twist fibrous rope that never broke, and so he was able to tie the end of it directly to the horn.

SADDLE RIGS

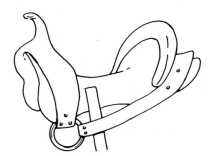 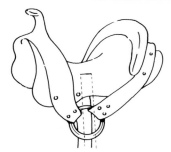 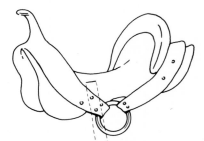 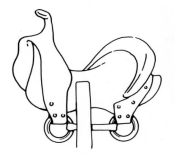

SPANISH SINGLE RIG   **THREE-QUARTER SINGLE RIG**   **CENTER-FIRE RIG**   **DOUBLE RIG**

Saddle

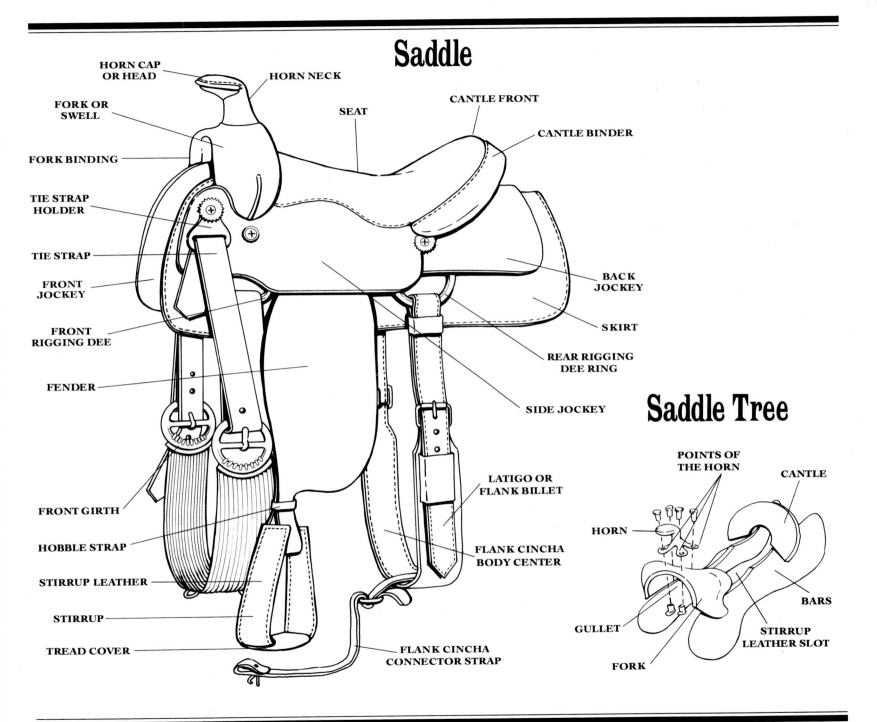

HORN CAP OR HEAD

HORN NECK

FORK OR SWELL

SEAT

CANTLE FRONT

CANTLE BINDER

FORK BINDING

TIE STRAP HOLDER

TIE STRAP

FRONT JOCKEY

BACK JOCKEY

FRONT RIGGING DEE

SKIRT

REAR RIGGING DEE RING

FENDER

SIDE JOCKEY

FRONT GIRTH

LATIGO OR FLANK BILLET

HOBBLE STRAP

STIRRUP LEATHER

STIRRUP

FLANK CINCHA BODY CENTER

TREAD COVER

FLANK CINCHA CONNECTOR STRAP

Saddle Tree

POINTS OF THE HORN

CANTLE

HORN

BARS

GULLET

STIRRUP LEATHER SLOT

FORK

SADDLE BLANKETS are placed under the saddle when riding. They absorb perspiration and make the saddle fit better by compensating for irregularities in the horse's back. This 30″ × 60″ Tex Tan blanket has a whipstitched border. $6.75.

MASSACHUSETTS HORSEMAN E. O. KIMBALL rides "King's Marigold" in July 4th festival. His black hand-carved saddle is set off by a long, silver-studded sarape and matching tapaderos.

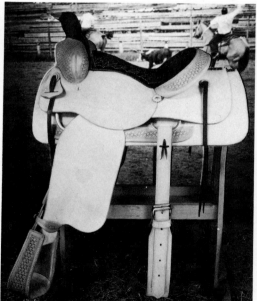

DESIGNED FOR barrel racing, Tex Tan's hand-tooled Speedy features a 14½″ rust suede seat and white buckstitching. $695.

ALL-AROUND SADDLE, Tex Tan's Tough Nut has a bullhide-covered tree, bullhide wrap on the fork and horn. $775.

TEX TAN'S DEEP-SEATED Golden Cutter is accented with silver conchas, floral tooling, and stitching. $970.

36

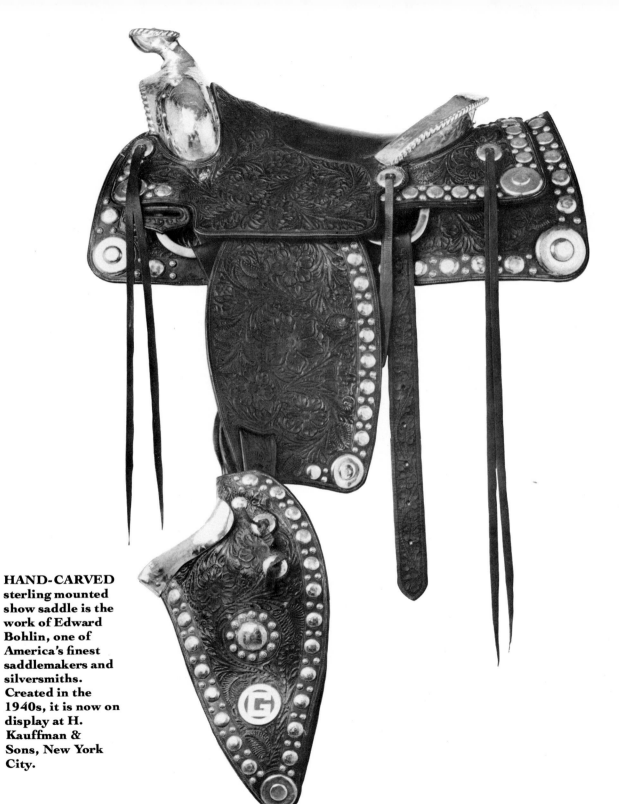

HAND-CARVED sterling mounted show saddle is the work of Edward Bohlin, one of America's finest saddlemakers and silversmiths. Created in the 1940s, it is now on display at H. Kauffman & Sons, New York City.

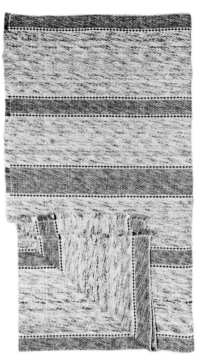

SADDLE BLANKET by Tex Tan is gray with bright stripes, 100 percent washable cotton. 30″ × 60″. $8.50.

INDIAN DESIGNS, stripes, and fringe highlight Tex Tan's cotton and rayon blanket. 30″ × 30″. $16.50.

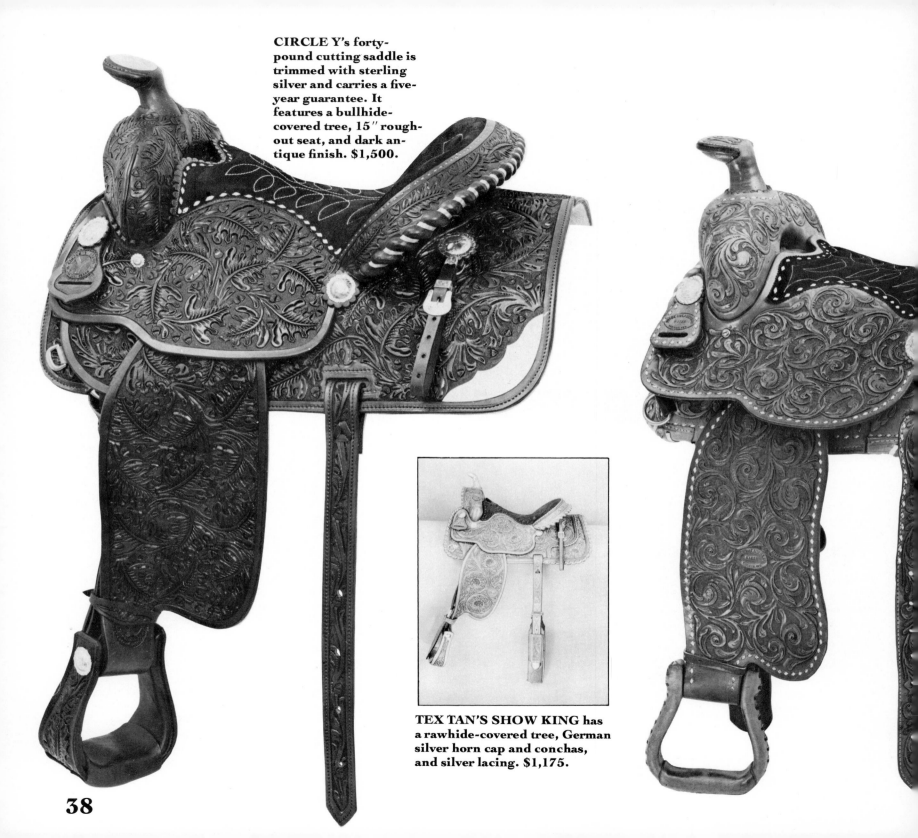

CIRCLE Y's forty-pound cutting saddle is trimmed with sterling silver and carries a five-year guarantee. It features a bullhide-covered tree, 15″ rough-out seat, and dark antique finish. $1,500.

TEX TAN'S SHOW KING has a rawhide-covered tree, German silver horn cap and conchas, and silver lacing. $1,175.

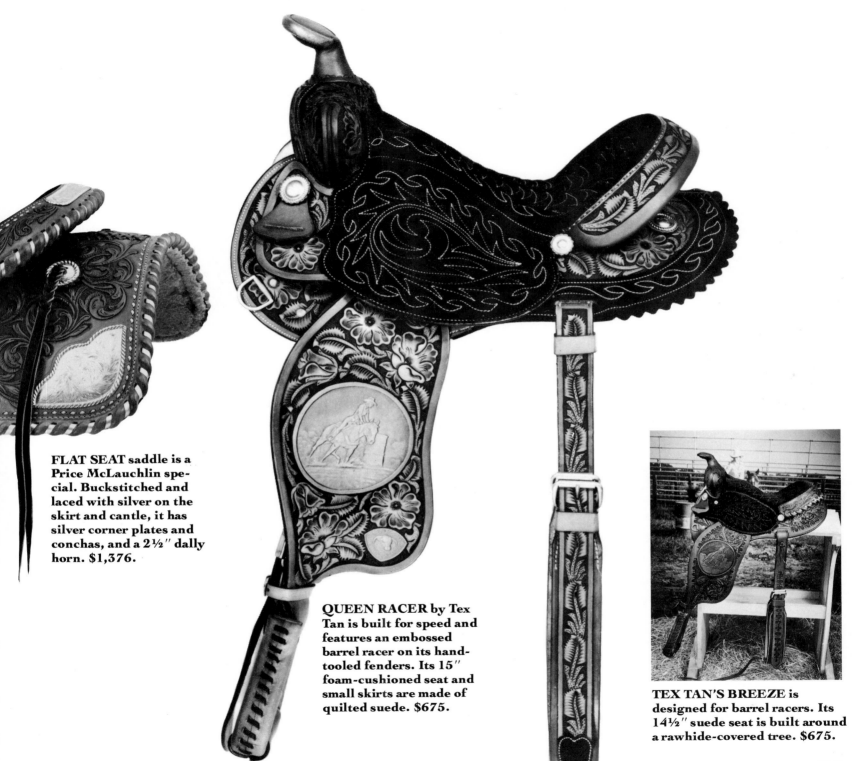

FLAT SEAT saddle is a Price McLauchlin special. Buckstitched and laced with silver on the skirt and cantle, it has silver corner plates and conchas, and a 2½″ dally horn. $1,376.

QUEEN RACER by Tex Tan is built for speed and features an embossed barrel racer on its hand-tooled fenders. Its 15″ foam-cushioned seat and small skirts are made of quilted suede. $675.

TEX TAN'S BREEZE is designed for barrel racers. Its 14½″ suede seat is built around a rawhide-covered tree. $675.

39

HOW TO SELECT A WESTERN SADDLE

There are so many different types of Western saddles that the first-time buyer (and the second and third-time buyer as well) is apt to throw up his hands and settle for the first one he is shown. Nevertheless, the right saddle is as important to a rider's safety as it is to his pleasure, and there are some basic facts you should know before setting out for the local saddler.

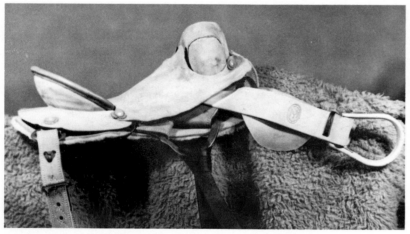

BOB BLACKWOOD's bronc saddle has a bullhide-covered tree, a full ¾" double rigging, and latigo-lined billets. $595.

Types of Saddles

The size, weight, and style of a saddle will depend on what that saddle is used for. A roping saddle, for instance, will be wide and heavy, with a low fork to reduce leverage against the horn and the horse's withers, and a low cantle to permit quick dismounting. A saddle used for pleasure riding will be small and light, with a high cantle for extra comfort. A show saddle will be elaborately outfitted and highly ornamental. All Western saddles are designed for a specific purpose, and before you buy one, you should decide on the type of riding you plan to do.

Saddle Quality

A saddle is only as good as its tree and for centuries the best trees have been those covered with rawhide. The rawhide is soaked in water and then, while still wet, is stretched over the tree to shrink and dry. The result is a tree that is both strong and resilient: strong enough to withstand an enormous amount of wear and tear, and resilient enough to adjust to the movements of the horse. Cheap trees, however, are often covered with little more than a bit of cloth and can easily damage the horse's back. They are unable to withstand shock and will break under minimal pressure.

Finding a Reliable Dealer

Before you buy a saddle, ask the saddler if he will allow you to return or exchange it if it does not fit properly. A saddle is an important and expensive piece of equipment, and since it is usually purchased by approximate measurement rather than by actual try-on, you must be allowed to correct your mistakes. However, if you buy your saddle on sale or at an auction, be prepared to keep it.

Caution: When buying a secondhand saddle, it is always safer to deal with a reputable saddler than with a "friend" at the stable. The saddler will check the saddle thoroughly to make sure it is sound and will stand behind the sale.

How to Measure Your Horse for a Saddle

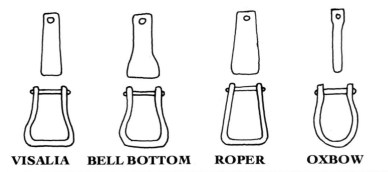

Stirrup Styles

VISALIA	BELL BOTTOM	ROPER	OXBOW

GETTING THE RIGHT FIT

FOR THE RIDER

Fitting the rider is a matter of selecting the proper seat size. Make sure you sit in the saddle and try it out before you buy it. Never rely on past experience. All manufacturers size differently and you may require different sizes in different models. Whatever you do, do not accept a bad fit. Today's saddles come in a wide range of sizes and styles and you can afford to be choosy.

FOR THE HORSE

A saddle should distribute the rider's weight evenly over the horse's back and should *never* touch the horse's spine. It should not put pressure on the horse's withers or pinch them, and should allow the horse's loins and shoulders to move freely. When a saddle fits properly, the bars lie flat on the horse's back (just behind the shoulder blades) and do not tip to one side or another; the gullet clears the horse's back by at least one finger when the rider is mounted, and by two fingers when he is not.

The best way to ensure a proper fit is to take the horse directly to the saddle shop. However, if this is impractical, you can do the next best thing: Make a template of his back and take it with you when you make your purchase. To make a template, you will need four strips of thin, pliable wire about thirty-six inches long, four sheets of cardboard, a pencil, and a pair of scissors. Here's how to do it:

1. Place one piece of wire across the horse's back, at the withers, and bend it to the shape of his body.

2. Carefully lift the wire off the horse and place it on a sheet of cardboard.

3. With a pencil, trace the shape of the wire onto the cardboard. You will now have a pattern of your horse's back at the withers. Cut it out.

4. Repeat steps 1—3 with the three remaining strips of wire, placing a strip every four inches.

When your saddler puts the four patterns together, he will have a facsimile of your horse's entire back and will be able to fit him correctly.

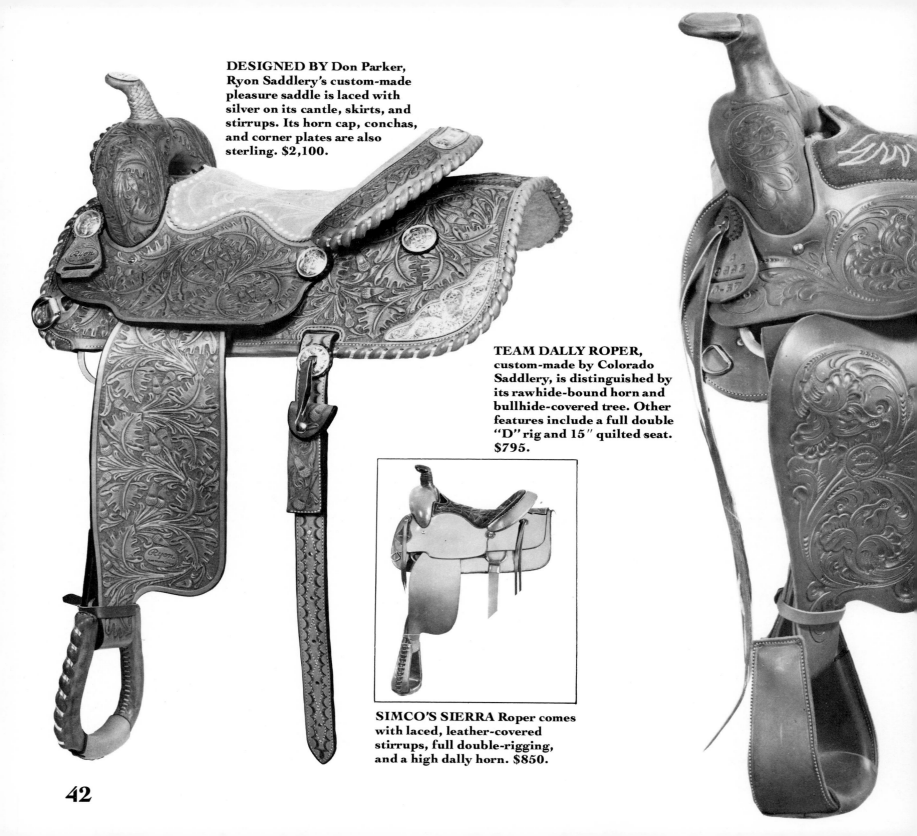

DESIGNED BY Don Parker, Ryon Saddlery's custom-made pleasure saddle is laced with silver on its cantle, skirts, and stirrups. Its horn cap, conchas, and corner plates are also sterling. $2,100.

TEAM DALLY ROPER, custom-made by Colorado Saddlery, is distinguished by its rawhide-bound horn and bullhide-covered tree. Other features include a full double "D" rig and 15″ quilted seat. $795.

SIMCO'S SIERRA Roper comes with laced, leather-covered stirrups, full double-rigging, and a high dally horn. $850.

42

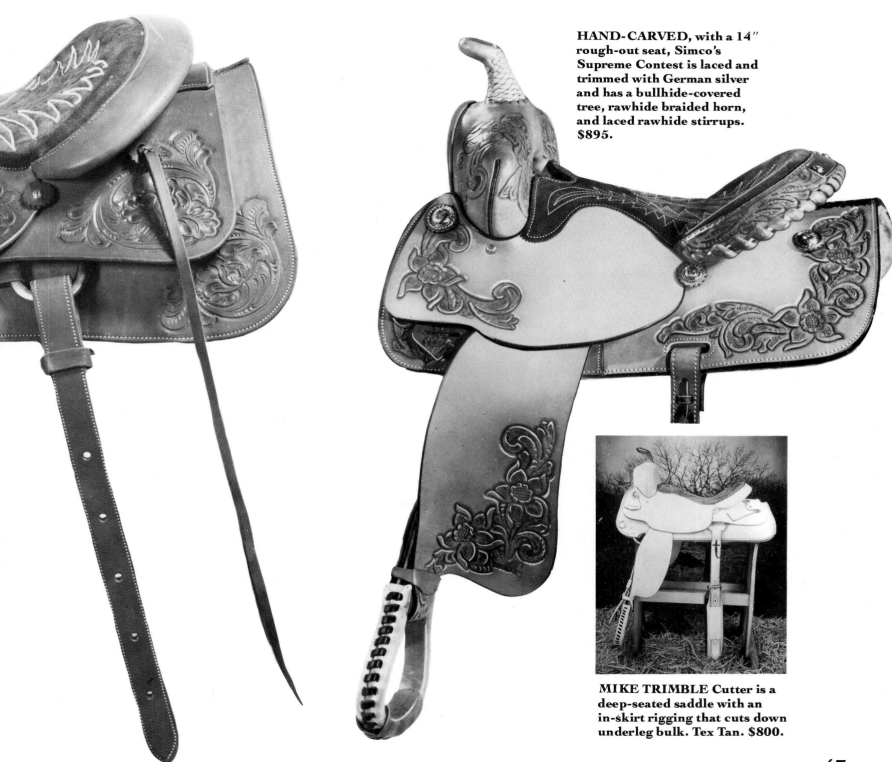

HAND-CARVED, with a 14″ rough-out seat, Simco's Supreme Contest is laced and trimmed with German silver and has a bullhide-covered tree, rawhide braided horn, and laced rawhide stirrups. $895.

MIKE TRIMBLE Cutter is a deep-seated saddle with an in-skirt rigging that cuts down underleg bulk. Tex Tan. $800.

ALL ABOUT LEATHER

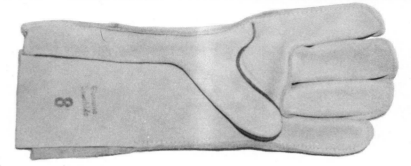

Leather is a strong, flexible material made from animal pelts that have been cleaned and tanned. The pelts of larger animals, such as horses, cows, and buffalo, are called "hides." Those of smaller animals, such as goats, sheep, pigs, calves, deer, and reptiles, are called "skins." (Pelts from large calves or small breeds of cattle, however, are "kipskins.")

How Leather Is Made

The pelts are cleaned and all hair, flesh, and fat is removed. To prevent them from stiffening and decomposing, they are "tanned," treated with either vegetable tannins from the barks of trees or with chromium salts. The first, and longer, of the two methods is called "vegetable tanning," and produces a firm, water-resistant (but not water-repellent) leather that can be carved and decorated. This type of leather is usually used for saddles. The second method,

called "chrome tanning" or "chemical tanning," produces light, pliant (but strong) garment leathers used for gloves, suits, and coats.

When the tanning has been completed, the leather is dyed and given either a suede finish or a smooth or embossed grain finish. This final process is the one that endows the leather with its tone and texture.

Types of Leather

BUCKSKIN Imported mainly from Canada and Latin America and used for clothes, gloves, and high-quality shoes.

CALFSKIN A fine-grained, durable, and scuff-resistant leather used for gloves, handbags, boot uppers, and linings.

COWHIDE, steerhide, and bullhide. Tough, long-wearing leathers used for boot and shoe soles, heels, saddles, harnesses, horse collars, straps, and handbags. Of all the leathers, cowhide is the

most useful. Thinned down, or *split*, it is used for gloves, belts, and clothing.

GOATSKIN and kidskin. Used for fine leather goods, including handbags. Kid is one of the softest, sturdiest, and most pliable leathers.

HORSEHIDE and buffalo-hide. Tough leathers used for shoes, gloves, belts, handbags, and luggage.

KANGAROO The strongest of all leathers, used for boots.

OSTRICH The only leather made from the skin of a bird, used for fine boots, hand-

bags, and wallets.

PIGSKIN Characterized by large pores from which the bristles have been removed, it is used for saddles, harnesses, gloves, and wallets.

SHEEPSKIN and lamb-skin. Skins with the wool left on, they are used for coats, boots, hats, and gloves.

AQUATIC ANIMALS (seals, sea lions, walruses, sharks, whales, alligators, and crocodiles). Used for boots, handbags, belts, and billfolds.

SNAKESKIN Highly tex-

tured skins from the lizard, python, and cobra are used for high-priced boots, belts, and handbags.

ALL-AROUND saddle from Price McLauchlin (*opposite*) features an unusual basket-weave design and comes with a full double rig, Texas dally horn, and leather-laced stirrups. $900.

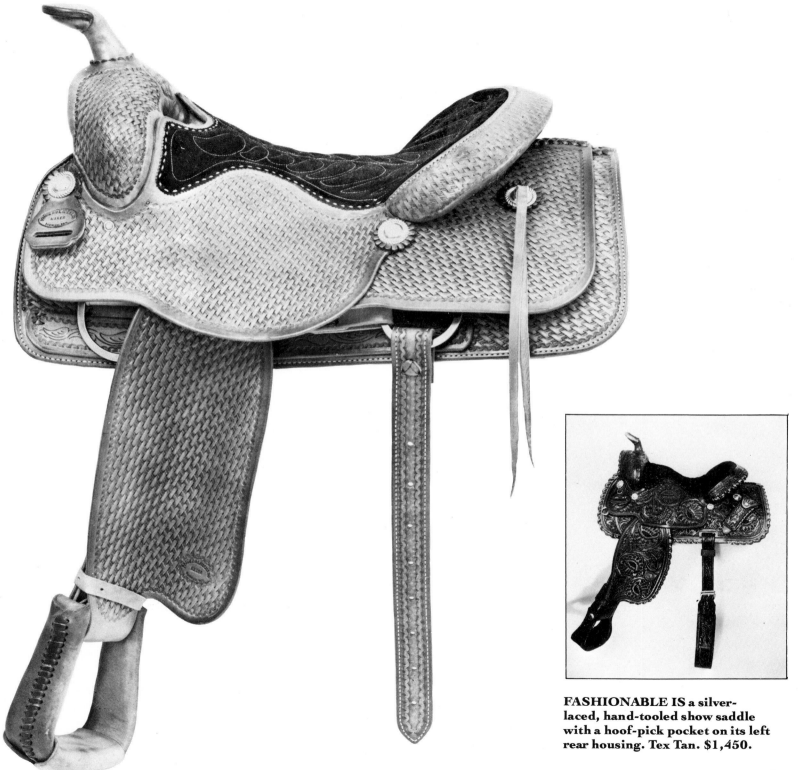

FASHIONABLE IS a silver-laced, hand-tooled show saddle with a hoof-pick pocket on its left rear housing. Tex Tan. $1,450.

A GLOSSARY OF WESTERN HORSES

THE QUARTER HORSE Originally bred in the Thirteen Colonies, this peerless cow horse is known for his spirit, stamina, intelligence, and obedience. A short, stocky animal — the fastest horse in the world over one-quarter-mile distances — he has a calm, gentle nature and is the favorite of rodeo cowboys and barrel racers.

THE ARABIAN HORSE The world's oldest and purest breed of horse, the Arabian was brought to North America by Cortez and was the ancestor of the Western cow pony. A beautiful animal, with slender limbs and a graceful, delicate head, he is noted for his energy and courage, is well suited to endurance contests, and makes a fine cutting horse.

THE MORGAN HORSE An American breed tracing back to one single stallion, Justin Morgan, who was foaled in Vermont in 1793, the Morgan horse is handsome, versatile, and fast. A champion harness racer, whose fancy gait also made him a popular coach horse, he works hard, learns quickly, and has superb "cow sense."

THE SPANISH BARB One of the world's oldest breeds, the Spanish Barb was born in ancient Persia and centuries later was brought to the Barbary States of North Africa by the Moslems. Small, sensitive, and highly intelligent, he came to the New World with the Spaniards and played a dominant role in the development of the Southwest. Thanks to his short back, dense bone structure, and compact size, he is an exceptionally fine athlete as well as a superior cow horse.

THE APPALOOSA An unusual-looking animal with dark brown or black spots, white-rimmed eyes, and striped hooves, the quiet, sensible Appaloosa is one of America's most popular horses and is a strong competitor in all rodeo events and endurance competitions. Brought to Mexico by the Spanish, the breed was eventually adopted by the Nez Percé Indians who inhabited the Palouse River region of Washington. The name "Appaloosa" comes from the word "Palouse."

THE PAINT and the PINTO Horses with promi-

nent, bright-colored patches are called paints or pintos (Spanish for "a mixture of colors"). If the animal is white with black patches, he is known as a piebald; if his patches are any other color, he is a skewbald. Pintos are noted for their toughness and endurance, and because of their natural camouflage coloring have always been great favorites of the North American Indians.

THE PALOMINO A bright golden mount with a long silver mane and tail, the spectacular palomino — the Golden Horse of the West — has always been featured in movies and parades, and is used extensively as a stock horse, Western pleasure horse, and trail horse.

THE ALBINO The bearer of kings, military heroes, and movie stars, the dazzling albino is a pure white horse with a white mane and tail, who is used primarily for pleasure riding. Unfortunately, many horsemen consider the animal a freak of nature and believe that his light eyes and pink skin are signs of weakness.

JEANS

One hundred and thirty years ago, a Bavarian immigrant named Levi Strauss found fame and fortune as the world's leading cowboy couturier. Having landed in America with little English and even less money, Strauss turned a small pushcart into a giant conglomerate and changed the dress code of an entire nation. His story is the story of jeans.

Like many another forty-niner, Strauss set out for California to look for the pot of gold at the end of the ledger sheet. He was hoping to sell canvas for covered wagons and tents, but soon discovered that wagon covers and tents were not exactly hot items. "Should have brought pants," the miners told him, "pants don't wear worth a hoot in the diggins." Strauss took the hint, folded his tents, and turned them into the roughest, toughest work pants in the West. He called his product "overalls," the miners called them "Levis," and for years bookkeepers have called them money in the bank.

Soon after his success with canvas, Strauss found an even rougher and tougher fabric, and began making his pants from a cotton that was loomed in Nîmes, France. It was called "serge de Nîmes" or "denim" for short, and blue denim came about when Strauss insisted on using an indigo dye to maintain uniformity of color. (The name jeans was derived from "Genes," the heavy denim pants worn by the sailors of Genoa, Italy. Sailors in Dhunga, India, also wore denim pants, known as dhungarees.) Shortly after the Civil War, Levis were shipped from California to Texas and proved so comfortable in the saddle that they were quickly adopted by working cowboys.

Blue denim Levis were guaranteed to "shrink, wrinkle, and fade," and were custom-tailored in a most ingenious way: Cowboys, miners, and farmers put them on and then jumped into a watering trough; when the pants dried, they fit. They fit so well, in fact, that they outsold every other type of pants in the West and, with their matching jackets, became the cowboy's unofficial uniform. In 1976, in honor of this country's bicentennial, a pair of Levis was placed in the permanent collection of the Smithsonian Institution.

Strauss's original models were not very different from the jeans of today. They had tapered legs, bright orange stitching, and copper rivets at all the stress points. The rivets are still in their original positions. With two exceptions: the back-pocket rivets, which had to be removed because they were scratching saddles and school furniture, and the crotch rivet, which disappeared when a Levi Strauss executive crouched too long before a blazing campfire.

TOUGH, INEXPENSIVE, and durable, jeans and jackets have been the cowboy's unofficial uniform for over a hundred years.

LEVI STRAUSS's canvas jeans are in the Smithsonian Institution, Washington, D.C.

LEVI STRAUSS & COMPANY, the "cowboy's tailor," made the jeans worn by these early cattlemen.

IN 1873 Levi Strauss and Jacob Davis, a Nevada tailor, patented their new invention: copper rivets used as reinforcements for pants pockets.

J. W. DAVIS.
Fastening Pocket-Openings.
No. 139,121.   Patented May 20, 1873.

Witnesses
Inventor

LEVI'S
Look for the RED TAB

America's Fir

52

ON LEVI'S TRADEMARK, two horses try to pull apart a pair of pants.

MINERS and farmers were the first Americans to wear Levi pants.

BILLBOARD AD, circa 1940.

EARLY AD shows 1886 version of two-horse trademark.

IN 1976 this Levi jean suit became part of the Smithsonian's Americana Collection.

53

WESTERN JEAN STYLES

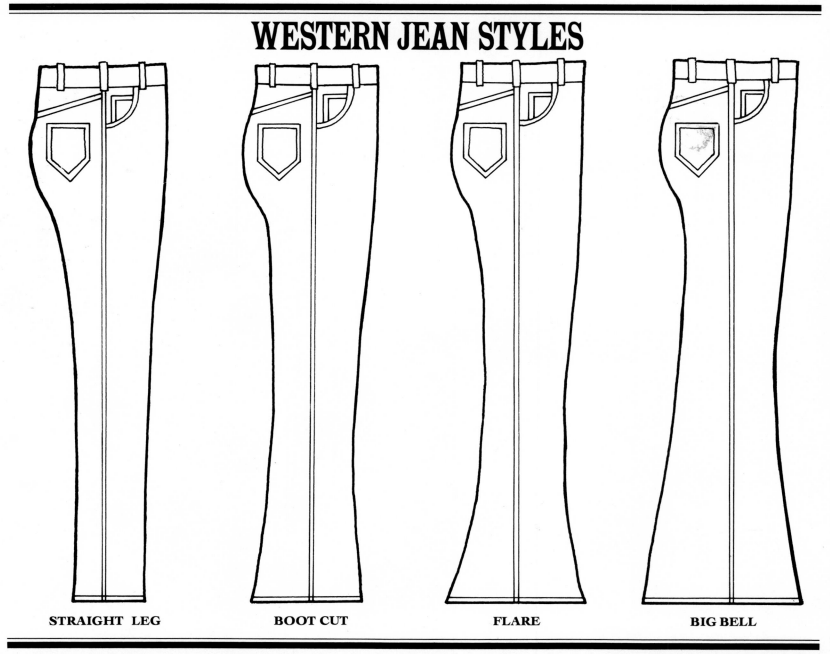

STRAIGHT LEG   BOOT CUT   FLARE   BIG BELL

Preceding page from left to right: **Cutter Bill specials in men's and ladies' sizes. Le Poché jeans with Rolls-Royce monogram in gold lurex, $35; Sasson straight-leg jeans, $35; State of Texas jeans, $30; Le Poché's Cutter Bill jeans embroidered with gold lurex, $42; Sheik jeans with button-through back pocket, $32; Cutter Bill's high fashion Western jeans, $30; Sheik straight-leg jeans, $32.**

"NO FAULT" jeans and jacket by Wrangler are 100 percent cotton SanforSet. Jeans, $18; jacket, $25. (*opposite*)

COWBOYS AROUND THE WORLD

In the hundred or so years since he first appeared on the Western frontier, the cowboy has made the transition from American hero to universal symbol. His rugged image has managed to transcend language barriers, national boundaries, and cultural differences, and from Picadilly Circus to Mid-Eastern oil fields few can resist the opportunity to try on a bit of the Old West.

PRINCE CHARLES (*left*) and Prince Andrew of England donned their best Western suits, ties, and hats for a 1977 visit to Canada's annual Calgary Stampede, one of the world's top rodeos.

NIKITA KHRUSHCHEV received a hot dog and a cowboy hat during a 1959 United States tour.

MICKEY MANTLE (*third from left*), surrounded by "international cowboys," hails from Oklahoma. Though he came to the rescue on the baseball diamond, his heart remains true to the spirit of the Plains.

ACCESSORIES

Because the early cowboy spent so much of his time in the saddle, he seldom, if ever, wore jewelry. Jewelry — rings, chains, pendants, bands — tended to catch on his riding equipment and on bull horns, and the man who got himself so entangled might pay dearly for his vanity. What the cowboy did have, and what he prized, were silver-mounted spurs and bits, and Mexican-style conchas, which he attached to his spur straps. The concha, Spanish for "shell," is a metal or silver disk that is mounted on leather by means of a loop or button on its back. It can be extremely simple or, when stamped or engraved with floral designs, highly ornate. Later on, when the cowboy began to compete in horse shows and rodeos, he emblazoned his saddle, bridle, belt, hatband, and chaps with dozens of these disks, and with silver mountings in other shapes — rectangles and diamonds — as well. The cowboy, incidentally, bought his silver first from the Mexicans and then from the Navaho Indians. The Navahos, who learned silversmithing from the Mexicans, copied a great many of the Spanish designs, among them the concha and the naja. The naja, which looks like an inverted crescent, and which the Indians later incorporated into the "squash blossom" necklace, was an ancient Moorish amulet that was meant to ward off the evil eye. The Spanish used to hang it on the horse's headstall, and when the cowboy saw it on the Mexican mounts, he too adopted the custom.

Today, with time and money at his disposal, the cowboy is likely to own more jewelry than did his predecessors. The items he favors are engraved silver shirt tips, boot ornaments, lighter covers, and money clips. The braided leather bolo ties he wears with his colorful shirts are usually accented with silver tips and jeweled slides, and his leather saddlery and accessories are not only studded with conchas, they are branded — with sterling silver monograms.

Even if you knew nothing of the cowboy's history, you could learn a great deal about him by looking at his accessories: at his bandannas, his bolo ties, his jewelry, and his decorative pieces for the home. Although all these items are colorful and imaginative, none is completely frivolous and without real significance. Even steer horns used as wall ornaments or elaborate snuffboxes reflect the cowboy's life and work. The fact that many of the cowboy's accessories are made of leather and silver is also an important point. Although both these materials are expensive and beautiful to look at, they are also strong and extremely durable, and are not subject to the whims of fashion.

THE COWBOY'S ACCESSORIES are very much like the cowboy himself — stylish, flashy, unusual, but practical.

BANDANNAS from H. Kauffman & Sons come in many patterns, a dozen colors. $2.50 each.

BANDANNAS

Working outdoors in all kinds of weather, the cowboy had to protect himself from the elements. One of his most effective defenses was the bandanna, a large cotton handkerchief that he folded diagonally and knotted around his neck. Worn with the knot in the back, the bandanna could be pulled up over his nose and mouth whenever he was exposed to dust, wind, or sleet. It could also be tied around his head to keep his ears from freezing, or tied around his hat to keep it from blowing away in a strong wind. The bandanna was one of the most versatile accessories the cowboy owned and he put it to many different uses: When he wanted to drink from a stream, he would spread it out over the water and let it filter out mud and dirt; when he was very hot, he would wet it down and wear it on top of his head; in an emergency, he could use it to tie a calf or a steer, and, if he hurt himself, he could turn it into a sling or a bandage.

Originally, the bandanna was a native of India, a silk handkerchief whose dotted pattern was applied by a process known as "bandhnu," or "tie-dye." Brought to Europe by the Portuguese in the sixteenth century, it later made its way to the southern United States, where it was manufactured in cotton for Negro farmworkers. Cowboys, who adopted it, bought it in blue and bright red and loved the touch of color it added to their wardrobes.

CARTIER LUGGAGE from Ryon Saddlery. *Clockwise from top:* small suitcase, $960; overnight bag, $640; large suitcase, $1,200; carryall, $420.

HEAVY side leather briefcase from Cutter Bill features a snaffle bit handle and hand-tooled oak-leaf design. $350.

STITCHED and welted roping gloves from Neiman-Marcus Red River Collection are made of natural deerskin. $25.

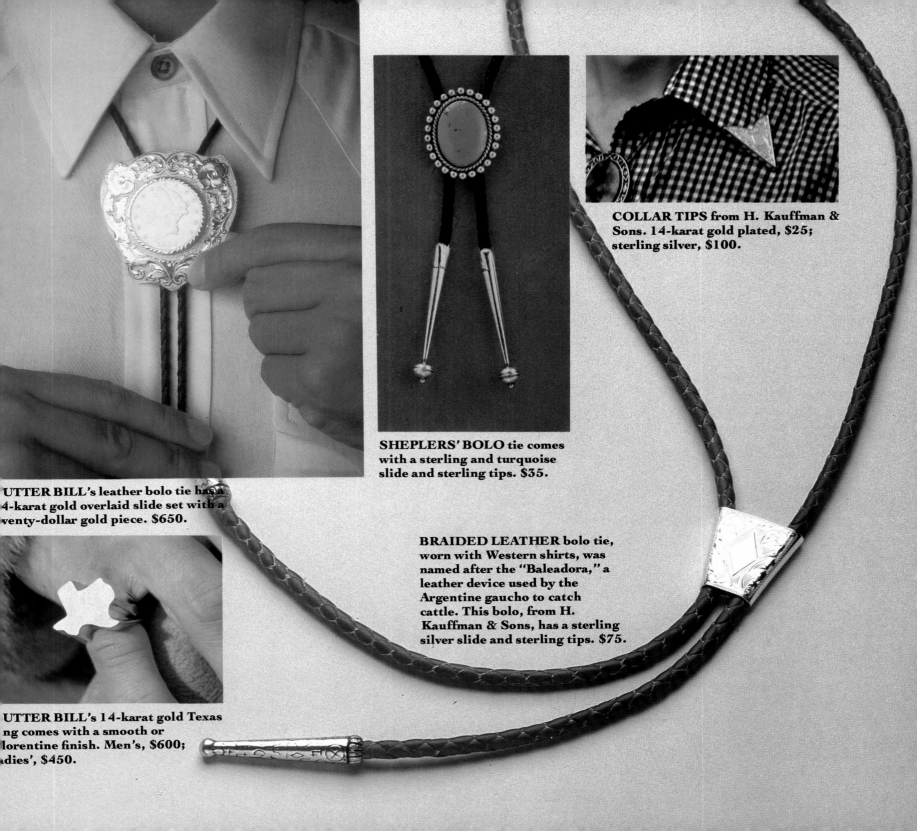

COLLAR TIPS from H. Kauffman & Sons. 14-karat gold plated, $25; sterling silver, $100.

SHEPLERS' BOLO tie comes with a sterling and turquoise slide and sterling tips. $35.

UTTER BILL's leather bolo tie has a 14-karat gold overlaid slide set with a twenty-dollar gold piece. $650.

BRAIDED LEATHER bolo tie, worn with Western shirts, was named after the "Baleadora," a leather device used by the Argentine gaucho to catch cattle. This bolo, from H. Kauffman & Sons, has a sterling silver slide and sterling tips. $75.

UTTER BILL's 14-karat gold Texas ring comes with a smooth or florentine finish. Men's, $600; ladies', $450.

HOW TO CARE FOR WESTERN SILVER

Good silver will last a lifetime, but only if it receives proper care and attention. To maintain its luster or restore its original brightness, follow this simple advice.

Wipe off dust and grime after every wearing.

To remove tarnish, use a liquid polish containing white French chalk. (Polish leaves a thin film of wax on the surface of the silver that protects it from the chemical effects of smudges and fingerprints.) Apply the polish to the silver with a soft cloth (a towel, an old T-shirt, or a bit of muslin) wrapped around your finger. Pat it into grooves and into hard-to-get-at places in the mountings.

If your silver is mounted on tack or on a belt, a boot, or a pair of chaps, apply the polish with a cloth-covered toothbrush. The toothbrush will give you more control over the application and will prevent the polish from running into the leather. If the polish does run, be sure to wipe it off quickly and thoroughly.

Silver polish is harmful to leather and must not be allowed to sink into its pores.

After you have finished cleaning the silver, polish it with a soft cloth to bring up its luster. The best type of polishing cloth is a piece of muslin that has been impregnated with a very fine grade of French chalk. Cloths that contain red jeweler's rouge are fine for freestanding silver, but will discolor leather and should not be used on mounted items.

Never paint silver with clear nail polish to keep it from tarnishing. Eventually, the polish will scratch, and tarnish will discolor the exposed surfaces, but not the lacquered ones. The result will be a highly unattractive mottled look.

Never use "silver-dip" on leather and silver combinations. A chemical cleaning compound, silver-dip was developed in Germany and is sold here under a number of brand names. It will disintegrate leather and, if left on too long, will blacken it beyond recall.

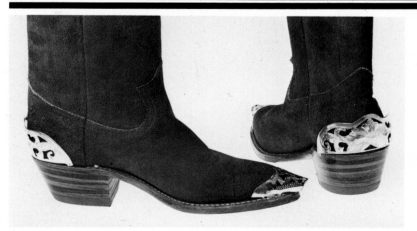 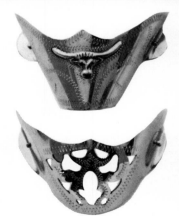 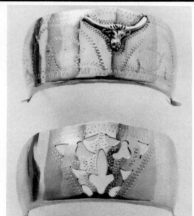

BOOT TIPS and heel guards from H. Kauffman & Sons. Rhodium-plated tips, $15 pair; guards, $15 pair. In sterling, each $150 pair.

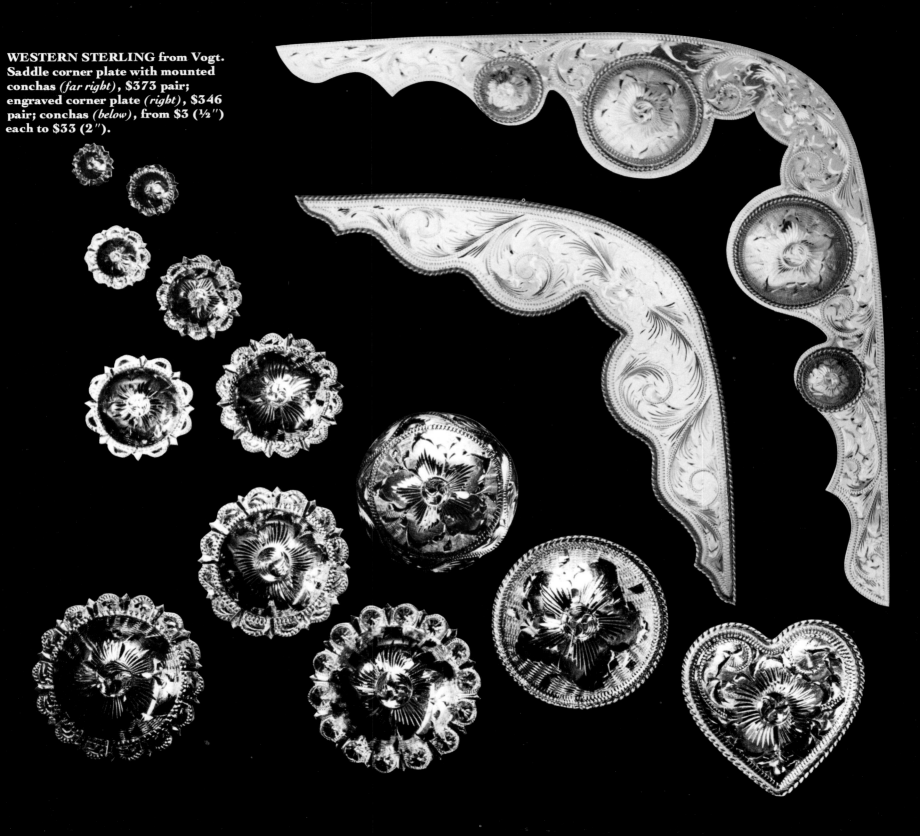

WESTERN STERLING from Vogt. Saddle corner plate with mounted conchas *(far right)*, $373 pair; engraved corner plate *(right)*, $346 pair; conchas *(below)*, from $3 (½″) each to $33 (2″).

JEWELER'S GLOSSARY

Before you invest in a silver buckle, or in any type of Western jewelry, you should know the meanings of the following terms:

ALLOY A mixture of two or more metals.

BASE METALS Copper, zinc, brass.

EMBOSS To stamp a raised design onto a piece of jewelry with a machine.

ENGRAVE To cut a design, by hand, into the surface of a piece of jewelry.

FINE SILVER Commercially pure silver. Contains no alloys.

GOLD 24-karat gold is pure gold. The term "karat" is a measure of fineness. If the gold content of an object is less than 10 karat, the object cannot be represented as karat gold.

GOLD FILLED Gold equivalent of Silver Overlaid. A very thin layer of gold joined to a bottom layer of base metal. Required by law to be identified by the term "Gold Filled" or "GF" plus a karat mark, e.g., "14K GF." When sterling silver is used as the bottom layer, the article will be marked "sterling 10K," giving the false impression that solid gold, rather than a thin layer of gold, is used.

NICKEL SILVER, also called "German silver." An alloy of nickel, zinc, and copper. Contains no silver. A hard, inexpensive metal that retains a shine and does not scratch or tarnish.

NU-GOLD Manganese bronze. A durable and inexpensive gold substitute.

OVERLAY Any decorative figure, scroll, brand, or lettering soldered onto an object. Not to be confused with Silver Overlaid.

PRECIOUS METALS Silver, gold, platinum, palladium.

SILVER OVERLAID A thin sheet of sterling bonded to a base metal backing. Usually contains less than 10 percent sterling silver and may not, by law, be stamped "sterling."

STERLING SILVER An alloy containing 92½ percent pure silver and 7½ percent copper. (Proportions fixed by law.) Rigid, durable, and expensive. Products stamped "sterling" have both a resale and a salvage value.

Courtesy, Tom Taylor

ENGRAVED STERLING letters to mount on saddlery or clothing. Vogt. ¾" letters, $8 each; ⅞", $9; 1", $10; 2", $27.

HAND-CARVED photo album by Tom Taylor is fitted with 14-karat gold and sterling silver nameplates and corners. $1,500.

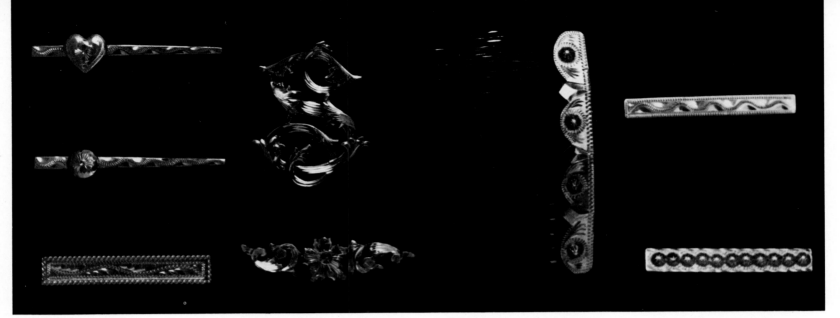

STERLING SILVER adornments from Vogt. Bar pins, $18 each.

HAND-ENGRAVED brooch *(top)*, $29; bar pin *(bottom)*, $15.95.

TORTOISE HAIRCOMB, 3″ wide, with engraved Western motif. $29.

ENGRAVED BAR PINS. Linear motif, $13; circular motif, $16.

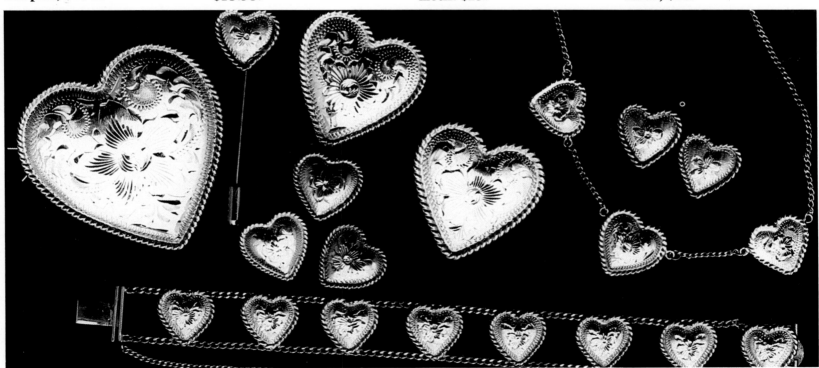

ROPE-EDGED heart jewelry from Ryon Saddlery is sterling silver. *From left to right:* barrette, $35; stickpin, $9; scarf pin, $18; buttons, $6.50 each; cuff buttons, $29 pair; necklace, $30; pierced earrings, $13; bracelet, $70.

VOGT's sterling silver snuff-can lid has a rope-edge initial space. $59.

STERLING snuff-can lid from Vogt. Also available with gold horsehead. $59.

SPUR ASHTRAY comes in chrome or blue steel. Bob Blackwood. $15.

VOGT's sterling lighter cover has spiral motif. $65.

STERLING lighter case. Vogt. $70.

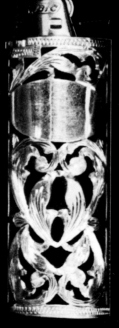

BIC lighter in sterling case from Vogt. $70.

FILIGREE lighter cover in sterling silver from Vogt. $65.

PERSONALIZED sterling money clip (top) and lighter case from Ryon Saddlery. Each $70.

SHEPLERS' genuine steer horns are highly polished and trimmed with leather-look vinyl. Mounted and ready to hang. $11.99.

NATURAL SHEARLING seat cover *(below)* from Sheplers fits almost any car seat. Installation instructions are included. $40.

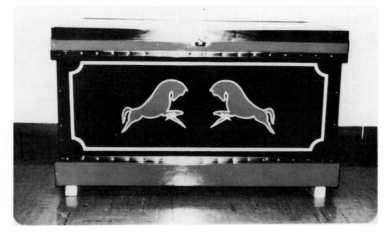

PERSONALIZED HARDWOOD tack trunks from Warner's have stainless steel top and edge molding. 38½″ × 24″ × 22″, $425; 32½″ × 18″ × 18″, $395.

MOVIE COWBOYS

The movie cowboys who carried the spirit of the West to the four corners of the earth were more than silver nitrate and celluloid. They were men of sterling character and unparalleled sincerity. Their minds were pure, their hearts were true. They stood straight and tall, and though they talked little, they always spoke the truth. Courteous to women, kind to children, and friends to all in need, they fought for law and order and *never ever* fired first. We shall not see their like again.

William S. Hart

**Roy Rogers
Dale Evans**

Lash La Rue

Hoot Gibson

Gabby Hayes

Hopalong Cassidy (William Boyd)

Gene Autry

Rex Allen

Will Rogers

Tom Mix

SPURS

When man first started to ride a horse, he had to find ways of making his mount obey him. He soon discovered that by placing a bit in the animal's mouth, he could control its direction and make it come to a halt; and that by kicking the animal in the side with his leg, he could make it move forward and accelerate. However, there were times when even the most sustained kicking failed to rouse the horse to action, and it was for times such as these that the spur was invented.

The first spurs, or "prycks," were long metal prods that attached to the backs of the rider's boots. Eventually, a small spiked wheel, known as a "rowel," was added to the end of the prod, and when this rowel dug into the horse's side, it quickly accomplished its purpose. In fact, the immediacy of the horse's response made the spur an indispensable part of the rider's equipment, and in the West it was said that a cowboy would sooner appear in public without his pants than without his spurs.

These spurs that the cowboy valued so highly (in truth, they were one of the great delights of his life) were adapted from the silver inlaid "Chihuahuas" worn by the Mexican vaqueros. The Mexicans, like the Spaniards, loved elaborate riding gear, and their spurs not only had huge eight-inch rowels, but an assortment of chains and pendants that clanked against the stirrups whenever they moved. Such spurs, of course, were not meant to be walked in, and were actually so unwieldy that they could not be put on until the vaquero was safely in the saddle.

The first American-made spurs were much simpler than their Mexican counterparts. To begin with, the Texas cowboy wanted a spur that he could walk in — not one that he had to keep putting on and taking off every time he mounted and dismounted. Secondly, since his horse was very valuable to him, and since he used his spurs more to threaten than to harm, he did not want to use any implement that had a sharp, cutting edge. The result was a spur with a small (two inches or less) blunt-edge rowel that proved to be extremely popular almost everywhere in the West. Everywhere but in California. The California cowboy continued to wear Mexican-style spurs, and to this day is much more Latin in his style of riding and style of dress than his Texas brother.

BELIEVED to have been worn first by Assyrian horsemen, spurs were one of the great delights of the cowboy's life.

PARTS OF THE WESTERN SPUR

Spurs are used to make horses move forward and are worn on the back of the rider's boots. The *heel band* slides onto the counter of the boot and is held in place by the *spur strap*, which buckles across the instep. For years, cowboys have argued over the buckle: Should it be worn on the inside of the foot or on the outside? Worn on the outside, it is more comfortable and is less likely to brush against the horse and inadvertently urge him on.

A spur with a straight heel band is called a *straight-button spur;* one with a band that curves upward is a *raised-button spur.* The *spur strap* and the *heel chains* are both attached to the *spur button*, which may be stationary or swinging. A swinging button is less apt to press against the rider's ankles. The heel chains, worn under the arch of the boot, were supposed to anchor down the spurs, but were basically noisemakers, and are seldom seen today. *Heel straps,* which also serve as anchors, are still worn (mostly by broncobusters), but the weight and shape of the spur are usually sufficient to keep it in its proper place.

There are three basic types of *shanks: straight shanks, raised shanks,* and *drop shanks.* The majority of riders prefer drop-shank spurs, but raised shanks are popular with broncobusters and with tall riders who have difficulty spurring because their legs hang down below the horse's sides.

On the upper part of the shank, there is often a rounded *chap hook,* which keeps the back of the rider's chaps from catching on the *rowel.* The rowel is the small wheel at the end of the shank that is used for prodding the horse. In the early days, small metal pendants called *jinglebobs* were attached to the rowel pins and, as they bounced against the rowels, they made bright, jingling sounds that delighted the cowboy.

Spur

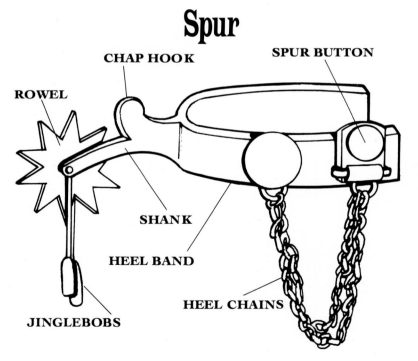

CHAP HOOK

SPUR BUTTON

ROWEL

SHANK

HEEL BAND

HEEL CHAINS

JINGLEBOBS

ROWELS

5-POINT

6-POINT

9-POINT

20-POINT

16-POINT

SAWTOOTH

10-POINT

7-POINT STAR

5-POINT STAR

SHANKS

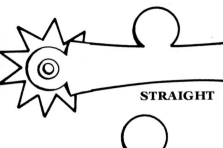
STRAIGHT

HALF-DROP

FULL-DROP

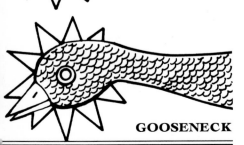
GAL-LEG

GOOSENECK

CHILD'S SPUR by Renalde, Crockett & Kelly (RC&K). $30.

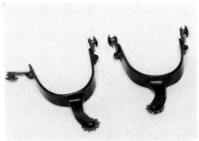

GAIL PETSKA barrel racer's spur by Bob Blackwood. $35.

STAINLESS STEEL spur; 2½″ shank, 1″ rowel. RC&K. $60.

RC&K STEEL roping spur with brass buttons, rowel. $45.

RC&K steel spur has 1¼″ heel band. $55.

RC&K CLIP-ON spur is chrome-plated steel. $27.50.

HANDMADE SPURS, available in stainless or blue steel, come with brass buttons, rowels, and shank tips. Brass letters are $2 apiece; brass bars on the shank and heel band are $10 extra. Ryon Saddlery. $44.

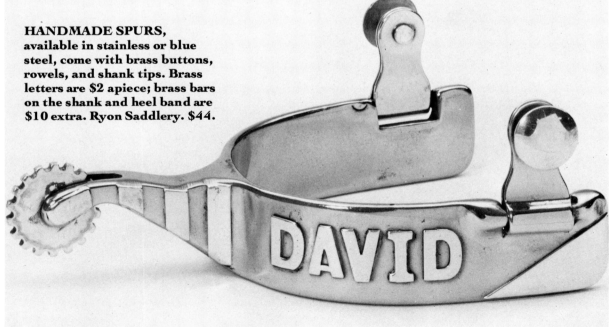

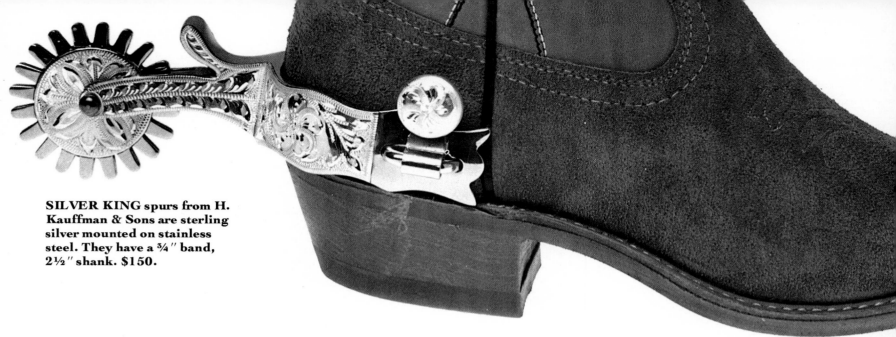

SILVER KING spurs from H. Kauffman & Sons are sterling silver mounted on stainless steel. They have a ¾″ band, 2½″ shank. $150.

ENGRAVED ALUMINUM SPUR from RC&K. $35.

ENGRAVED RC&K SPUR is sterling silver mounted on stainless steel. $195.

STERLING MOUNTED spur with tie-down button, 5-point rowel. RC&K. $195.

RC&K STERLING mounted cutting horse spur has blunt-edge rowel. $195.

HAND-ENGRAVED spurs *(right)*, personalized with gold Old English initials, are made with a sterling silver overlay on stainless steel. Ryon Saddlery. $275.

ENGRAVED ALUMINUM spur with 2½", 16-point rowel from RC&K. $35.

RC&K STERLING mounted spur has ¾" band, shamrock rowel. $195.

STERLING MOUNTED RC&K spur with 1" band, 5-point star rowel. $195.

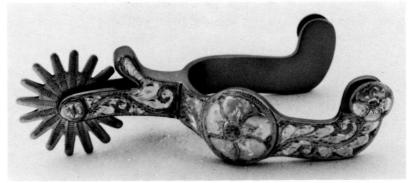

RC&K RAISED BUTTON, sterling mounted spur has 1½" concha. $250.

WHO WAS WHO

It is only natural that a section of our country as large as the West produced characters that were larger than life. Here are some of the immortals.

JUDGE ROY BEAN: Fat, unkempt, and illiterate, the Kentucky-born Bean moved to the West Texas town of Langtry where he had himself appointed Justice of the Peace. He then set up a saloon and, for the next twenty years, held court in the bar. He was, he said, the only law west of the Pecos, and, dispensing his unique brand of justice, once fined a corpse forty dollars for carrying a gun.

BILLY THE KID: A teenage cattle rustler and gunslinger who killed his first man at the age of twelve, William H. Bonney was shot down by Sheriff Pat Garrett after playing a leading role in the notorious Lincoln County cattle war. Although he was only twenty-one when he died, he was responsible for the deaths of at least twenty-one men.

BLACK BART: A poetry-writing bandit who liked to leave samples of his work at the scenes of his crimes, Bart, alias C. E. Bolton, held up twenty-eight stages before the Wells Fargo Company tracked him down through a telltale laundry mark. In the years that followed, Bart's poems were written in San Quentin.

BUFFALO BILL: Pony Express rider, Indian fighter, cavalryman, and scout, William F. Cody won his colorful nickname by killing four thousand buffalo for the Kansas Pacific Railroad. In 1883 his touring Wild West Show gave the public a firsthand look at cowboys and Indians and made his expert marksmanship and flamboyant personality famous throughout the world.

CALAMITY JANE: A hard-drinking, tobacco-chewing frontierswoman with a heart of gold, Martha Jane Canary became a heroine when she helped nurse victims of a South Dakota smallpox epidemic. A skilled rider and expert shot, she supposedly got her nickname by threatening that calamity would befall any man who dared to offend her.

WYATT EARP: The hero of countless TV and movie Westerns, the celebrated marshal of Dodge City started out as a stagecoach driver, buffalo hunter, and surveyor. In 1881 he, his brothers Morgan and Virgil, and Doc Holliday took part in a famous gun battle at the O.K. Corral and shot down three notorious cattle rustlers in the space of a minute. Earp died in Los Angeles in 1929 at the age of ninety.

CHARLES GOODNIGHT: An Indian fighter and scout who became one of the most famous cattlemen in the West, Colonel Goodnight laid out the Goodnight-Loving Trail, established the first ranch on the Texas Panhandle, founded one of the area's first schools, and was credited with the invention of the chuck wagon.

JOHN WESLEY HARDIN: The son of a Methodist preacher, "Wes" never believed in turning the other cheek, and by the time he was twenty-two he had killed thirty-seven men in "self-defense." He later studied law while serving a twenty-five-year prison term, but after passing the bar was unable to pass the local saloon, where he was gunned down by Sheriff John Selman.

WILD BILL HICKOK: A frontier scout and quick-draw man who became one of the greatest gunfighters in the West, Hickok was a feared and respected lawman. It is said that he killed only in self-defense and made it a point of honor to give all his victims funerals.

DOC HOLLIDAY: A gunslinging dentist from Baltimore who was fond of killing, drinking, and cheating at cards, John Henry Holliday was deputized by the Earp brothers and once saved Wyatt's life in a shoot-out. His most notable battle, however, was with tuberculosis, which forced him to give up his dental career and ended his life when he was only thirty-five.

FRANK and JESSE JAMES, COLE and BOB YOUNGER: In 1866 the James boys and their kinfolk, the Youngers, decided to go into business together. The business? Bank and train robbery. Crime paid very well until 1876, when the Youngers were captured and sent to prison and each of the James brothers had a five-thousand-dollar price put on his head. Frank eventually turned himself in, was acquitted by the court, and ended up as a racetrack starter; Jesse died at home, shot in the head by a friend.

BAT MASTERSON: Cool, handsome, and debonair, Bat Masterson was a Western fashion plate who never went out without a derby hat. After a brief stint as a lawman in Dodge City, he tried his luck at gambling and eventually ended up in New York City as a topflight sportswriter for the *Morning Telegraph*.

ANNIE OAKLEY: An expert markswoman who learned to shoot at the age of nine, Annie spent seventeen years as the star of Buffalo Bill's Wild West Show. Because she could puncture a playing card five or six times before it fell to the ground, free tickets with holes punched in them are known as "Annie Oakley's."

FREDERIC REMINGTON: A graduate of the Yale School of Fine Arts and an easterner, this superlative artist traveled extensively throughout the American and Canadian West and recorded the frontier drama in vivid, action-filled paintings that have become classics.

CHARLES MARION RUSSELL: A self-taught artist who was born in St. Louis, Russell developed an early love of the West and, at sixteen, moved to Montana to work as a ranch hand. His paintings of Western life are based on his own experiences and are so accurate in every detail that he is known as the "Cowboy's Artist."

BELLE STARR: The glamorous saloonkeeper heroine of so many movie Westerns was actually a petty horse thief who ran a livery stable in Dallas and later retired to a riverside cabin where she dispensed tea and sympathy to itinerant bad men.

SHERIFF PAT GARRETT brings Billy the Kid to justice.

SUITS

In the Old West the major social event of the year was the cowboy dance. This eagerly awaited formal brought out the whole countryside and seldom lasted less than two or three days. Catered by one of the big ranches, it was a noisy and colorful gathering and was the one occasion on which the cowboy wore a suit. A real suit. Not the two-piece denim or canvas outfit that braved the brush country but a coat, vest, and trousers made of dressy blue serge or "gambler's stripe" (black wool or cotton, with thin white stripes running through it). The type of suit that demanded a necktie and made the cowboy look, in the words of one bystander, "plum civilized."

The suit, however, was a tame affair. Imported from New York or Philadelphia, it had no true individuality, no characteristics that we could call "Western." It was in the conventional European style of its time and looked very much like today's three-piece, single-breasted business suit. The Western suit, as we know it, did not actually come into being until just before World War I. Only then, when he had the time and money to socialize, did the cowboy put his ideas and his personality into his dress clothes.

The cowboy designed his suit, as he designed *all* his clothes, for strength and durability as well as for beauty. The coat and vest, though not worn as work garments, have the same stress-resistant yokes as his work shirts. The trousers, though not worn in the saddle, have all the features of riding pants: legs that are tapered on top (so they will not chafe the rider or catch on brush) and wide at the bottom (so they will fit over a boot); deep vertical pockets that are set high on the hip (so coins cannot fall out); rear pockets that are covered by flaps (so nothing can bounce out of them); and extra-wide belt loops that accommodate broad Western belts.

If the suit is casual, it will be made of sturdy polyester or gabardine; if it is more formal, it will be made of twill, worsted, or sharkskin. And it will come from one of the nation's best suit manufacturers — for when today's cowboy kicks up his heels, he demands the very best his hard-earned money can buy.

CUTTER BILL's Western World in Dallas caters to the urban cowboy (and girl). *From left to right:* brown and gray wool tweed jacket has Western yoke, piped sleeves, and lapels. The heather skirt, slit front and back, is accented with arrowheads. Condor. Sizes 5 to 13. Jacket, $90; skirt, $46; toast wool flannel suit by Cutter Bill is tailored with single point yokes and keystone belt loops. 38R to 46L, $425; navy Western blazer comes in cashmere/wool or camel's hair, $175. The full, button-front skirt is lined and made by Cutter Bill in gray and navy. 6 to 14, $75; Cutter Bill's own navy wool vest suit features banker's stripes, single point yokes, and keystone belt loops. 38R to 46L, $390.

RANCHER SUIT by Oleg Cassini is made of designer's new Saddle Suede fabric. $275.

SPRINGFIELD, a modified Western suit by Niver, is yoked only in the back. Under $150.

SHEPLERS' TEXTURED polyester stretch suit *(left)* has a two-button coat and lined vest. $99.

WESTERN SPORT jacket from H Bar C *(right)* features hacking pockets and an unusual vertical stitch pattern. $125.

SHARPLY PEAKED lapels and besom pockets accent this all-wool English twill jacket *(opposite)* by Country Britches. $265.

NUDIE *(top)*, a 76-year-old tailor from Brooklyn, is Hollywood's foremost Western designer. His clients include top TV and movie stars and rhinestone cowboys like this Nashville buckaroo.

SCULLY's glazed lamb blazers have two-button fronts, patch pockets, and unusual trim. The blazer at left and its matching five-button vest are embellished at the yoke and pockets with four rows of boot stitching.

CLASSIC WESTERN suit, complete with yoked shoulder and pockets, five-button vest, and keystone belt loops. H Bar C. $195.

azer, sizes 38 to 46R and L, $355; vest, sizes 38 to 46R, $130. Cognac azer at right has ostrich accents. His sizes 38 to 46R and L, $550; her zes 6 to 14, $500. All at Cutter Bill's.

RANCHER ART PERRY and his nine-year-old Morgan stallion dress up for California's annual Rose Parade. Perry's costume is a dazzling example of the Western showman's style and dash.

MR. AND MS. three-piece suits in striped blue polyester. The Ranchera for her, sizes 6 to 18, $115; the Rancher for him, sizes 36 to 46R and L, $145. By Lasso.

86

THE SQUIRE, Western formal from After Six (*opposite*), has satin lapels and satin-piped yokes, matching shirt, and string tie. $130.

H BAR C's Western shirt comes with glen-plaid bib, collar, and cuffs, matching bell-bottom ranch pants. $100.

SKIRT AND SHIRT from Salaminder with satin Rose of Texas applique. $150. Jacket by Above The Crowd. Price on request.

CHAR'S FRINGED jacket and pants *(opposite)* in blush Argentinian calf suede have old buffalo nickel button closings. Jacket, $250; pants, $250.

SALAMINDER's silky boot-length vest is hand-appliqued with prairie scenes and is available only at Cutter Bill's. $185.

WISHING WELL BRIDGE, oil painting by Richard McLean, depicts Miss Rodeo America contestants.

CHAPS

The Western movie horse was a paragon of virtue. Gentle, intelligent, well-mannered, you could always count on him to do the right thing at the right time. Away from the silver screen, however, he was a horse of a different color. Rub him the wrong way and, quicker than you can say Roy Rogers, he would step on you, throw you, and kick you when you were down. He might even bite you. (Catch Trigger doing *that*!)

Needless to say, such rude behavior can be hard on a rider's legs, and it does not do his britches any good either. For this reason the cowboy began wearing chaps, or leather leggings, over his pants and boots. They not only cut down his tailoring bill, they cut down his injuries. In fact, they offered protection against a great many things: against rain and snow and cold, against saddle sores, and, most particularly, against the dense and thorny brush of the Southwest. The word "chaps" itself is a Western abbreviation of the Spanish *chaparreras* (leg armor), which, in turn, comes from *chaparro* (evergreen oak). It was the chaparro, with its strong and treacherous branches, that produced a need for the chaparreras.

Like many good things in this world, chaparreras, or chaps, came about rather by accident. Spanish riders who flung animal hides over their saddles discovered that by folding those hides back over their legs, they could avoid cuts and bruises. It was a matter of one hide saving another, and the next step was inevitable: hanging the hide on the man rather than on the saddle.

The first American chaps were very much like Indian leggings: two separate leather shafts held together by a belt and decorated at the outside seam with long fringe. They were called "shotgun" chaps (because the two shafts resembled the two barrels of a double-barreled shotgun), and if they had no fringe they were simply "closed leg" chaps (because their sides were sewn, rather than laced, buckled, or tied together). In either case, they kept out snow and wind and were especially popular in the Northwest.

Down Texas way, the looser, cooler, batwing chaps were the thing. These snapped, or laced, together and opened easily when a cowboy got himself caught on a horse, a fence, or a saddle. For sheer razzle-dazzle, however, nothing could beat the long-haired fur "woolies." Made of angora goatskin, sheepskin, and even bearskin, they were great at shedding wind and water and were worn in blizzard country — Montana, Wyoming, and the Dakotas — and on Hollywood sound stages, where they managed to steal scenes from some of the biggest mink coats and chinchilla wraps in the business.

CHAPS PROTECT the cowboy's legs from saddle sores, from rain, snow, and cold, and from dense and thorny underbrush.

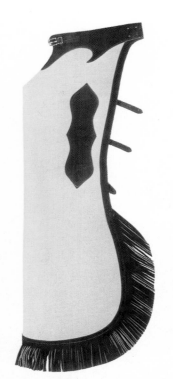

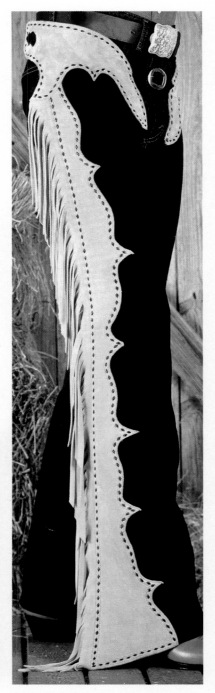

ACTION CHAPS for bareback riding. Rodeo Shop. $200.

CUTAWAY chaps for the arena. Rodeo Shop. $200.

SHEPLERS' show chaps *(left)* **with yoke, buckle closing. $110.**

RYON'S CUSTOM-MADE fringed chaps with your initials. Sueded leather, $300; top grain, $325; glove tan, $350.

STITCHED show chaps with yoke overlay. Sheplers. $165.

CUSTOM-FITTED chaps in smooth or rough-out calf from Cutter Bill. *From left to right:* black, straight-leg chaps with medium fringe, $175; two-color scalloped chaps with double fringe, hand-cut initials, $400; navy chaps with silver buckle, $275.

How to Measure Yourself for Chaps

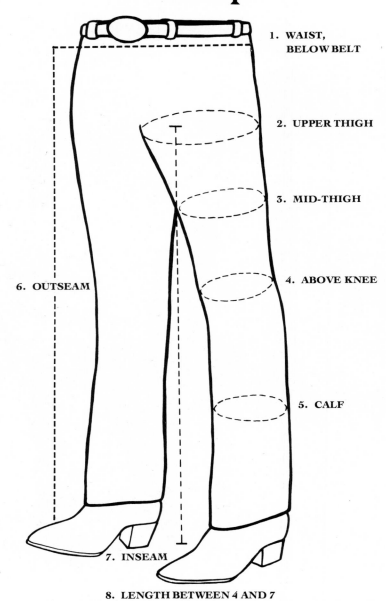

1. WAIST, BELOW BELT
2. UPPER THIGH
3. MID-THIGH
4. ABOVE KNEE
5. CALF
6. OUTSEAM
7. INSEAM
8. LENGTH BETWEEN 4 AND 7

CHAP STYLES

BATWING   **BATWING (Rear View)**

WOOLIE   **CLOSED LEG**

EQUITATION CHAPS (*opposite*) **in suede** (*left*) **$112; top grain, $137; glove tan, $163; batwing chaps** (*center*) **in suede, $108; top grain, $134; glove tan, $159; flower chaps** (*right*) **in suede, $117; top grain, $134; glove tan, $148. All from Cutter Bill.**

RYON'S CUSTOM CHAPS. *From left to right:* **Ladies Choice in suede, $140; top grain, $185; glove tan, $295; Ladies Champion (silver not included) in suede, $125; top grain, $145; glove tan, $185; Ladies All-Around in suede, $135; top grain, $155; glove tan, $195.**

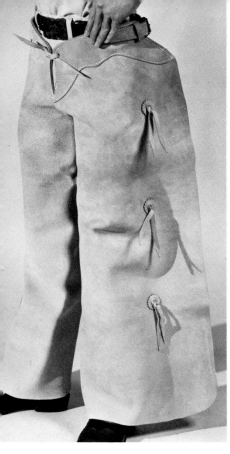

WOOLIES are custom-made from 4″ long wool fleece by Rogue Leather Co. Choice of colors, snap or zipper closings, back or front buckle. $200.

TEX TAN's split leather batwing chaps have adjustable leg snaps. $75.

FARRIER'S APRON ties in front. Tex Tan. $40.

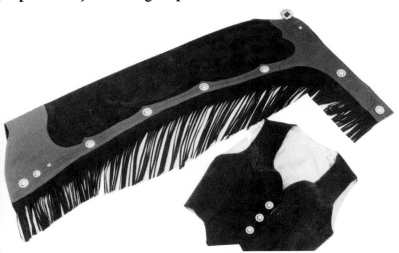

AR W's chaps and vest can be accented with 21 sterling silver conchas. aps, $135. Vest, $60. Small conchas, $6 each; large conchas, $12.

Entertaining Cowboy Style

Take one w-i-d-e open space and one slow-burning fire, add heaps of hot, scrumptious food, season with Western high spirits and southern hospitality, and you have the Texas barbecue, one of the world's most memorable culinary — and social — events.

Introduced to America by the French, the barbecue was originally a big, neighborly bash, a noisy and colorful outdoor feast at which a whole steer was roasted over a mesquite or hickory wood fire. The animal was spitted from "barbe" (whiskers) to "queue" (tail), and the food was served to the guests directly from the carcass. Over the years, however, the barbecue's menu has grown more varied, its service less primitive, and its cooking methods more sophisticated. Luckily, its atmosphere has remained as festive and uninhibited as ever, and if you plan to celebrate Texas Independence Day — or any other special day — the following, from Arthur Berwick, an actor, cook, and friend from the Longhorn State, will feed fifty hungry revelers.

Tips on Giving a Barbecue

Your menu should always include two choices of meats, such as beef and pork ribs, chicken and ribs, or beef and sausage. To be truly Western, of course, you really should include beef.

When cooking on a barbecue grill, place your meat 4 to 5 inches above the coals; when cooking on an open barbecue pit, your meat should rest 18 inches above the coals.

While the meat is cooking, baste it frequently with the marinade. Do not, however, coat it with the barbecue sauce until 5 minutes before it is done, since the sauce will cause the meat to burn.

Always have a good selection of pickles and relishes, such as dills, bread-and-butters, and sweet gherkins. Potato chips are also traditional, as is plain, ordinary, commercially packaged sliced white bread, called "light bread."

Although ranch coffee is traditionally brewed in an open kettle with a green stick resting on top (to keep the coffee from boiling over), any good bulk recipe for coffee will do.

Menu for a Texas Barbecue

Barbecued Beef
Barbecued Pork Ribs
Barbecued Chicken
Barbecued Polish Sausage
Ranch-style Beans

Potato Salad
Cole Slaw
Assorted Pickles
Potato Chips
Bread

Beer, Iced Tea, Soda, Ranch-style Coffee

BASTING MEDIUM

weak vinegar
salt
pepper
oil

NOTE: If you are not cooking over a wood fire but would like your food to have a hickory flavor, you may add a touch of "Liquid Smoke."

BARBECUE SAUCE*

2 cups chili sauce
¼ cup Worcestershire sauce
3 tablespoons Tabasco or hot pepper sauce
1 teaspoon mustard
¼ cup vinegar

Mix all ingredients together, then simmer for 10 to 20 minutes.

*There are as many recipes for barbecue sauce as there are ways to skin a cat. You can use your favorite or, if you don't feel like fussing, you can buy one of the very fine commercial brands now on the market.

BARBECUED BEEF

2 briskets of beef, choice, 5 to 7 pounds

Place beef on rack in an electric oven. Cook for 2¼ hours at 375°. Place on barbecue grill for another 45 minutes. Coat with barbecue sauce during last 5 minutes.

BARBECUED CHICKEN

12 chickens, quartered
½ cup salad oil
½ cup vinegar
1 teaspoon salt
½ teaspoon black pepper
2 tablespoons Worcestershire sauce
several generous dashes of Tabasco

Combine the oil, vinegar, salt, pepper, Worcestershire sauce, and Tabasco, and pour the mixture over the chicken. Allow the chicken to marinate for an hour or more, then grill it over the charcoal until the bones are loose and the juices run clear.

During the last 5 or 10 minutes, baste with barbecue sauce.

BARBECUED SAUSAGE

1 dozen Polish sausages
½ cup salad oil
½ cup vinegar
Tabasco to taste

Cut sausages in halves or quarters, then score them crosswise at 1-inch intervals. Brush with the oil-vinegar-Tabasco mixture and grill until brown and sizzling hot. Add barbecue sauce during the last 5 minutes of grilling.

BARBECUED RIBS

12—15 pounds of spareribs

Cut the ribs into 2-rib segments. Place them on a rack in a foil-lined pan. Bake for 45 minutes in a moderate (350°) oven. Transfer to outdoor grill for final crisping. Coat during last 5 minutes with barbecue sauce.

RANCH- STYLE BEANS

10 large cans (1 pound or more) pork and beans
3 large onions, chopped
1 bottle catsup
1 small jar mustard
2 cups brown sugar
½ cup vinegar
3 tablespoons cinnamon
1 teaspoon allspice
1 teaspoon Tabasco sauce
black pepper

Combine all the ingredients and place in a greased casserole. Bake for an hour or more in a moderate oven (350°) until beans have browned. Be careful not to burn.

POTATO SALAD

20 pounds boiling potatoes
1 pint mayonnaise
¼ cup prepared mustard
½ cup pickle relish
1 bunch celery, diced
salt and pepper
paprika
hard-boiled eggs

Peel, halve, and boil the potatoes, then allow to cool. Cube the potatoes, then combine with other ingredients. Dust with paprika and garnish with sliced hard-boiled eggs.

COLE SLAW

2 large cabbages, finely chopped
1 bunch carrots, grated fine
1 cup sour cream
2 teaspoons celery seed
¼ cup vinegar
ample black pepper
approximately 1 pint mayonnaise

Combine all ingredients, and add mayonnaise until the slaw has a creamy consistency. Refrigerate overnight.

HATS

On February 2, 1979, on a historic visit to the United States, Vice-Premier Teng Hsiao-ping, of the People's Republic of China, arrived in Texas and, according to the New York *Post*, "donned a cowboy hat with a red feathered hatband and opened the Round-Up Rodeo by circling the arena in a stagecoach." The next day newspapers around the globe carried a photograph of the premier in his new hat, and there was no mistaking the message: Far East had met Far West and a new era in world diplomacy had begun.

Next to the Stars and Stripes and the Statue of Liberty, the cowboy hat is America's most famous symbol. And, like all symbols, it speaks a universal language. To proclaim his friendship for West Germany, President Kennedy once said, "Ich bin ein Berliner." To proclaim his friendship for America, Premier Teng said nothing at all. He simply put on the hat that said "USA," and that one picture was worth a thousand words.

The story of the premier's hat has a second significance, less concerned with politics than with the family of man. Teng had mentioned that he was looking forward to the rodeo because it was similar to an old Mongolian sport. He was referring to a game of great intensity and speed—a war game, really—played over seven hundred years ago by Genghis Khan and his mounted horsemen. The Mongols who competed at this game wore hats with high crowns and wide brims that were strikingly similar to the Spanish and Mexican sombreros from which the cowboy hat evolved. Therefore, when Teng put on that Western hat, he was really putting on a small part of his own past.

How do we explain such coincidences, such kinship between two seemingly different cultures? The truth is that the Asian steppes and the Western plains are not so different after all. Though they are separated by continents, they share a similar landscape—a vast, open grassland with little natural shelter. In this harsh environment, both spawned a special race of men, professional riders who lived their lives on horseback and waged a constant war against the elements. Faced with similar problems, these men found similar solutions. They sought protection from the hot sun and the driving rain, from sharp winds and flying dust, under wide-brimmed hats, and they kept these hats cool by topping them with high crowns. Indeed, high crowns and wide brims were worn by many other men in their circumstances: by the Argentine gaucho, the Australian stockman, the Spanish cattleman, the Canadian Mountie, the Mexican vaquero. Their hats

AFTER the Western hat has been styled and shaped on a hand-carved wooden block, it is reduced to its final size with steam.

100

were the hallmarks of their proud professions, and they wore them with grace and great style.

The American cowboy, however, did more than just wear his hat, he put it to work. In his resourceful hands it became an all-purpose tool: a bellows to light his campfire, a whip to make his horse go faster, a prod to move a stubborn steer. Filled with water, it could be a drinking cup or a horse trough; placed on the ground, a pillow; waved in the air, a signal. For a man who traveled with a single pack, its versatility was a godsend. Wherever the cowboy went, his hat went with him. He wore it when he worked and wore it when he played. He wore it so frequently, in fact, that it became an extension of himself. Shaped by his personality, weathered by his experience, it was everything he was: tough, durable, resilient — unique.

The cowboy hat had more variations than Carter had oats (see Texas Talk, page 122). There were regional differences. The sun had a strong influence on style, and the more southerly the terrain, the wider the brim and the higher the crown. The steaming Southwest produced the ten-gallon hat, and though that outsize critter eventually became popular in the northern plains, northern hats generally had narrower brims and lower crowns than their southern cousins.

The Western hat was not made-to-measure but came off the shelf in black, brown, and light gray felt. (In Westerns, the good guys wore light hats and the bad guys wore dark hats so that the audience could tell them apart in the chase. In real life there were no such guidelines.) Crowns and brims could be found in every size and shape imaginable and hatbands were available in an endless variety of skins and feathers. But it was the cowboy himself who gave the hat its real individuality. By bending it, creasing it, curling it, and decorating it, he turned it into an original work of art — an American original that became a world legend.

HIGH FASHION felt hats from Resistol's Stagecoach Collection have fancy trims. Comstock *(left)*, $68. Mojave *(right)*, $68.

ESISTOL's avajo has 6½" rown, 3¾" rim, authentic urquoise and eather band. 90.

PESO features a copper-colored concha link band, 7" crown, 4" brim. Resistol. $74.

OP MONEY omes with fancy rosgrain band d binding, and feather. Resisl. $64.

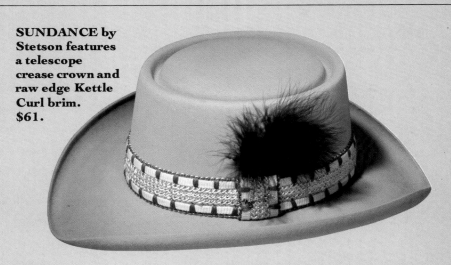

SUNDANCE by Stetson features a telescope crease crown and raw edge Kettle Curl brim. $61.

TETSON's ighland has 7" ullrider crease rown, 4" brim, randing iron in. $63.

LARGE FEATHER and black and white braided band enliven Outlaw by Resistol. $68.

Crease Styles

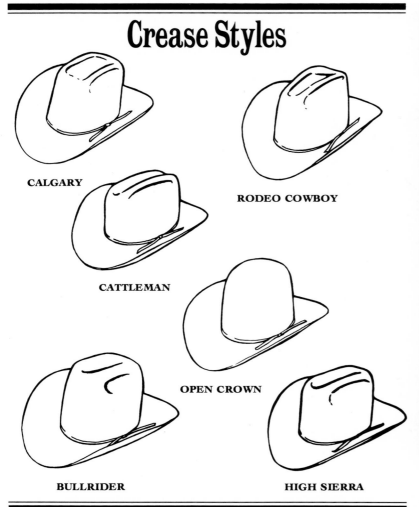

CALGARY

RODEO COWBOY

CATTLEMAN

OPEN CROWN

BULLRIDER

HIGH SIERRA

IN 1925 Stetson named a hat after one of America's most popular movie cowboys. The Tom Mix had a 7½" crown and 5" brim.

IN THE OLD WEST cowboys did their own hat creasing, and creases were generally regional. Southwesterners favored high crowns with three or four creases in the sides, while northwesterners wore their crowns flat. Today hats are made with certain standard creases *(above)*, but many retailers *(right)* do custom-creasing on the premises.

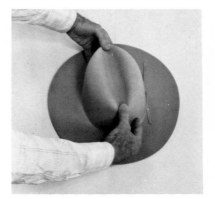

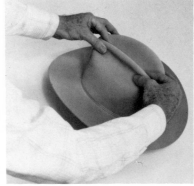

104

ORIGINAL of this Byer-Rolnick hat, modeled by Will Walters, was designed for Western film star Roy Rogers.

BYER-ROLNICK's Western-style hat with fancy feathers was worn by Errol Flynn in the Warner swashbuckler *Don Juan*.

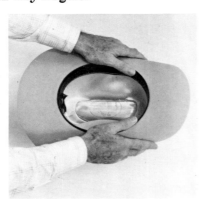

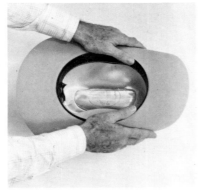

PIKES PEAK by Resistol is made of handwoven polyhemp fiber and has a hand-rolled brim. $25.

BLACK MESA with 6½″ crown and 4″ brim is made of handwoven Formosan fiber. Resistol. $27.

FINE-WOVEN, vented Toyo fiber is used for Resistol's Blue Range. $27.

UNUSUAL, ventilated rope weave, 7″ crown, 4″ brim, are featured in Resistol's Mesquite. $28.

RESISTOL's jute burlap Copper Creek is set off with an ostrich plume, braid hatband. $30.

HANDWOVEN of polyhemp, Resistol's Johnny Bull has a bound edge, matching band. $27.

FELT—The Heart of the Western Hat

While glorifying the cowboy's struggle against outlaws, outcasts, and outdoor living, the media have ignored another bane of his existence: headgear. The sad truth is that the early drover had almost as much trouble with his hat as he did with varmints. Made of the cheapest wool, it had no body whatsoever. The brim collapsed after one or two wearings, and if he wanted to see where he was going, he had to pin or tie it to the crown. It was not until the advent of felt that the cowboy was able to expand his field of vision. Felt revolutionized the Western hat. Strong yet lightweight, weather resistant yet smooth to the touch, it kept its shape and finish through endless wearings. Even today, the best Western hat is a felt hat, and here, with a little help from the Stetson Hat Company, is everything you need to know about the fabric and the finished product.

Felt is different from all other fabrics because its fibers are matted together rather than woven. It is made of short, single, animal hairs that have a natural tendency to "crawl," twist, and interlock when they are kneaded and manipulated in steam and hot water. Because each of its fibers interlocks in every direction with several other fibers, felt is much stronger than fabrics whose threads are woven either at right angles to one another or in parallel lines (and can therefore be torn apart along any straight line).

There are two types of felt hats: fur felt (medium or high priced) and wool felt (low priced). Fur felts are made chiefly of rabbit and hare, with beaver (the finest fur) and nutria topping the line. "Fur" in this case refers not to the long, coarse hair of an animal, but to its downy undercoat. Only this underfur has the barblike projections that lock the fibers together to make a strong felt.

Three factors determine the price of a felt hat: the quality of the fur, the quality of the trimming, the workmanship.

Fur comes in dozens of different grades of rabbit, hare, nutria, and beaver. Each has its own property of felting tightly or loosely, and the tighter the felt, the more "live" and shape-retaining the hat will be. The highest quality furs—those that command the highest prices—come from the backs of land animals and the bellies of water animals. Hats are also made from reclaimed fur (short stock) and synthetic fibers, but these lack the sheen, feel, and durability of the better furs.

Trimming, too, varies in type and quality. Satin linings cost more than cotton, just as fine leather hatbands cost more than synthetics.

Workmanship counts more than you think. The body of a hat may be rushed through the shrinking rollers just once, or it may be run through repeatedly, with constant inspection. It may also be "pounced" (shaved) once or repeatedly. And, since time is money, hats with special textures or special features cost more because more time is needed to produce them.

COUNTY SHERIFF by Resistol is beaver, has cord band. $55.

BAILEY's fur felt Country Swinger is topped by a 7″ crown. $51.

FUR FELT Quarter Horse by Bailey has a 7″ crown, 4″ brim. $55.

STETSON's Revenger has Tite telescope crown, raw edge brim. $52.

BEAVER TWISTER by Resistol comes with a 2-cord band, 7″ crown. $56.

WILD OATS by Bailey is fur felt, with a 7″ crown and 4″ brim. $55.

BAILEY's Big John comes in navy, rust, toast, and green felt. $51.

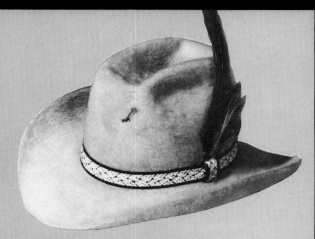

STETSON's Colter has bullrider crease crown, angora finish. $62.

SILK-LINED Dalworth by Resistol is beaver with a bound-edge brim. $55.

ORIGINAL Tom Mix hat by Stetson. Mix took dozens with him on personal appearance tours and presented them to local dignitaries.

BEAUMONT by Stetson features a Canadian crease crown. $63.

STETSON—The Boss of the Plains

What did Winston Churchill have in common with Buffalo Bill? The Duke of Windsor with General Custer? The King of Siam with Calamity Jane?

If you guessed Stetson, you're right on target. In little over a hundred years, the fabled Hat of the West has gone to the heads of kings and commoners, movie stars and superheroes, and even the United States Marines. How it got there is a success story so filled with clichés, it might have been dreamed by Horatio Alger.

In the late 1850s John B. Stetson, son of a master hatter from Orange, New Jersey, set out for the wide-open spaces (Missouri, at that time), hoping to find health and fortune. One of twelve children, Stetson had been frail and delicate from birth and was schooled only in his family's business. Although he was not expected to live past thirty, fate, that whimsical lady, stepped in and smiled at him. The rigors of the trail and the outdoor life not only restored his health, relined his lungs, and squared his shoulders, but inspired him to design a wide-brimmed, high-crowned hat that would shield a cattleman from rain and sun. Made of felt and called "The Boss of the Plains," it was an immediate success and changed the look of the West. Unlike its woolen predecessors, which quickly went limp and came tumbling down over the cowboy's eyes, the new hat kept its shape and wore beautifully.

The rest, as they say, is history. The Boss of the Plains and its successors sparked an industrial empire, achieved international fame, and made their creator's name a synonym for "cowboy hat."

LALOO

HIGH ROLLER

ARMY SERVICE

CARSON

CONGRESS

SAN AN

CARLSBAD

SOUTH

HATS from Stetson's 1925 catalog were "typical of the great outdoors."

STETSON'S NEW BREED: Chapparal *(right)*, $62; Comanche *(far right)*, $56.

Cody Outwits the Road Agents

It had become known in some mysterious manner, past finding out, that there was to be a large sum of money sent through by Pony Express, and that was what the road agents were after.

After [their] killing the other rider, and failing to get the treasure, Cody very naturally thought that they would make another effort to secure it; so when he reached the next relay station he walked about a while longer than was his wont.

This was to perfect a little plan he had decided upon, which was to take a second pair of saddle-pouches and put something in them and leave them in sight, while those that held the valuable express package he folded up in his saddle-blanket in such a way that they could not be seen unless a search was made for them. The truth was, Cody knew that he carried the valuable package, and it was his duty to protect it with his life.

So with the clever scheme to outwit the road agents, if held up, he started once more upon his flying trip. He carried his revolver ready for instant use and flew along the trail with every nerve strung to meet any danger which might confront him. He had an idea where he would be halted, if halted at all, and it was a lonesome spot in a valley, the very place for a deed of crime.

As he drew near the spot, he was on the alert, and yet when two men suddenly stepped out from among the shrubs and confronted him, it gave him a start in spite of his nerve. They had him covered with rifles and brought him to a halt with the words: "Hold! Hands up, Pony Express Bill, for we know yer, my boy, and what yer carries."

"I carry the express; and it's hanging for you two if you interfere with me," was the plucky response.

"Ah, we don't want you, Billy, unless you force us to call in your checks; but it's what you carry we want."

"It won't do you any good to get the pouch, for there is nothing valuable in it."

"We are to be the judges of that, so throw us the valuables or catch a bullet. Which shall it be, Billy?"

The two men stood directly in front of the pony-rider, each one covering him with a rifle, and to resist was certain death. So Cody began to unfasten his pouches slowly, while he said, "Mark my words, men, you'll hang for this."

"We'll take chances on that, Bill."

The pouches being unfastened now, Cody raised them with one hand, while he said in an angry tone, "If you will have them, take them." With this he hurled the pouches at the head of one of them, who quickly dodged and turned to pick them up, just as Cody fired upon the other with the revolver in his left hand.

The bullet shattered the man's arm, while, driving the spurs into the flanks of his mare, Cody rode directly over the man who was stooping to pick up the pouches, his back turned to the pony-rider.

The horse struck him a hard blow that knocked him down, while he half fell on top of him, but was recovered by a touch of the spurs and bounded on, while the daring pony-rider gave a wild triumphant yell as he sped on like the wind.

The fallen man, though hurt, scrambled to his feet as soon as he could, picked up his rifle, and fired after the retreating youth, but without effect, and young Cody rode on, arriving at the station on time, and reported what had happened.

He had, however, no time to rest, for he was compelled to start back with his express pouches. He thus made the remarkable ride of three hundred and twenty-four miles without sleep, and stopping only to eat his meals, and resting then but a few moments. For saving the express pouches he was highly complimented by all, and years afterward he had the satisfaction of seeing his prophecy regarding the two road agents verified, for they were both captured and hanged by vigilantes for their many crimes.

From *The Great Salt Lake Trail,* by Colonel Henry Inman and Colonel William F. Cody, pp. 193—98. Copyright, 1898, by The Macmillan Company, New York and London.

BRIDLES

A bridle is a leather harness that enables a rider to guide and control his horse. And if ever a horse needed guiding and controlling, it was the wild mustang of the American West. A descendant of the Spanish Arabian, the mustang was the fastest thing on four legs, and for sheer stubbornness and grit, there wasn't another horse who could touch him. Born of wandering strays, of runaways from the great Spanish herd, he grew up in the deserts of the Southwest, where he acquired incredible stamina and strength — ideal qualities for a cow pony. The cowboy took one look at him, saw his potential, and put him to work. But not before he had equipped his bridle with a portable torture chamber called a "bit."

The bit, a metal bar flanked by two side pieces, or "cheeks," is inserted into the horse's mouth and attached to reins that are held in the rider's hands. When the reins are pulled, pressure and pain build up in the mouth, and force the horse to comply with the rider's demands.

Although the Spanish did not invent the bit — it had been around for centuries — they found many ways of making it more lethal. The spade bit, which they passed onto the cowboy, had a spadelike projection in the center of the bar and could make a bloody mess out of any horse who refused to perform. The justification for this sort of cruelty was that cattle driving was an extremely dangerous occupation, and unless a horse could be trained to stop and turn at a moment's notice, the cowboy was in real trouble. Fortunately, the mustang was as smart as he was fast, and both horse and rider managed to emerge intact.

The happy ending may have been due to still another Spanish innovation: the "barrel roller," also known as a "cricket" or "taster." This was a small copper wheel attached to the center of the bar, and when the horse rolled it with his tongue, it made a soft, chirping noise. The horse loved the noise and the taste of the copper, and the roller not only entertained him but relieved his tension. It also relieved the monotony of the cowboy's job, for when the chirping combined with the jingling of his spurs and the clicking of his leathers, the range was filled with a sweet and wonderful music.

HIGHLY DECORATED silver-mounted bridles favored by Western horsemen were inherited from the Spanish colonists.

PARTS OF THE WESTERN BRIDLE

In the old days many Western bridles were homemade, and there were a great many variations in style and in the types of materials used. The rigging of the bridle could be extremely simple (i.e., the one-ear bridle) or it could have a full complement of equipment. If leather was not available, the cowboy might use woven horsehair, rope, or even wool.

The bridle is composed of three distinct parts: the headstall, the bit, and the reins.

THE HEADSTALL is made of leather and fits over the horse's head. It has a *crown*, which goes behind the ears; a *browband*, which rests on the forehead; two *cheekpieces*, which

catch the top rings of the bit; a *throatlatch*; a *noseband*; and a *curb strap*, which sits behind the lower lip and holds the bit in position.

THE BIT is the metal part of the bridle that is inserted into the horse's mouth. The *bar*, or *mouthpiece*, rests on the tongue; the two *sidepieces*, or *cheeks*, support the bar and line up at the corners of the mouth. The basic Western bit is a *curb bit*, which is roughly the shape of the letter "H." It has rings at the top, where it attaches to the headstall, and rings at the bottom for the reins. A *curb strap* or *chain* is usually attached to the top rings. It holds the bit in position and provides pressure on the jaws when the reins are pulled.

The horizontal bar has many variations in shape: a hump is called a *port*; a joint in the middle is a *snaffle*; a flat piece of metal is a *spade*. When stronger restraints are needed, the bar may be fitted with rings, rollers, chains, springs, and assorted lumps and bumps. If none of these works, a leather noseband called a *hackamore* (a bastardization of the Mexican *jaquima*) can be relied on to inhibit the horse's breathing whenever he disobeys.

It was fairly easy to tell where a cowboy came from by looking at his horse's bit. Texans, and most hands east of the Rockies, favored the curb bit. West of the Rockies, particularly in California, where the Mexican influence was strongest, the spade bit was preferred.

THE REINS are usually made from leather straps or braided rawhide strings, and are either "closed" or "open." Most Californians used *closed reins*, which were knotted together to form a short whip, or *romal*, at the end. California reins were often attached to the bit by small chains so that the horse would not chew them. In Texas, *open*, or *split*, reins were preferred. These were not joined together and fell to the ground as soon as the rider dismounted. The horse then stopped dead in his tracks and considered himself "tied." He would not move, since moving meant he would step on his own reins and trip.

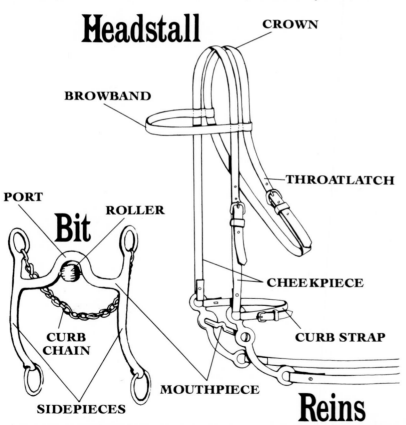

Headstall

CROWN

BROWBAND

THROATLATCH

PORT

Bit

ROLLER

CHEEKPIECE

CURB CHAIN

CURB STRAP

SIDEPIECES

MOUTHPIECE

Reins

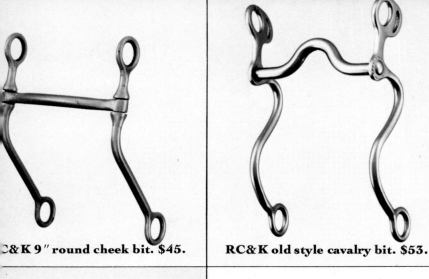

C&K 9″ round cheek bit. $45.

RC&K old style cavalry bit. $53.

RC&K loose jaw snaffle bit. $37.

PORT bit by RC&K. $42.

ADE port bit by RC&K. $69.

RC&K braided hackamore. $59.

RC&K flat cheek hackamore. $47.

ALUMINUM hackamore. RC&K. $37.

ERLING mounted RC&K bit. 5.

RC&K sterling mounted bit. $225.

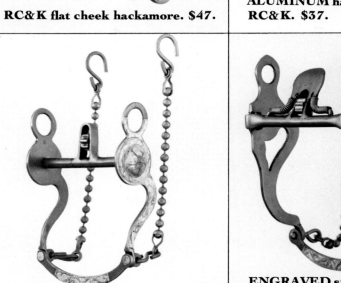

BIT with cricket. RC&K. $265.

ENGRAVED spade bit. RC&K. $265.

SIMCO. $217.	VOGT. $162.	VOGT. $153.*	VOGT. $173.	SIMCO. $217.
VOGT. $162.*	VOGT. $162.	VOGT. $162.	VOGT. $162.	VOGT. $162.
SIMCO. $239.	VOGT. $159.	VOGT. $162.	VOGT. $162.	SIMCO. $274.

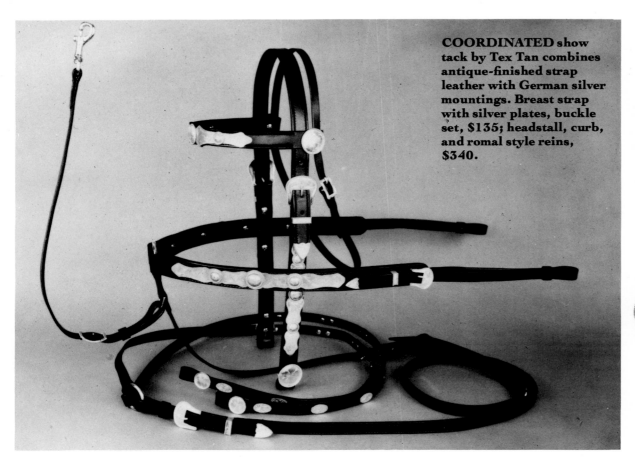

COORDINATED show tack by Tex Tan combines antique-finished strap leather with German silver mountings. Breast strap with silver plates, buckle set, $135; headstall, curb, and romal style reins, $340.

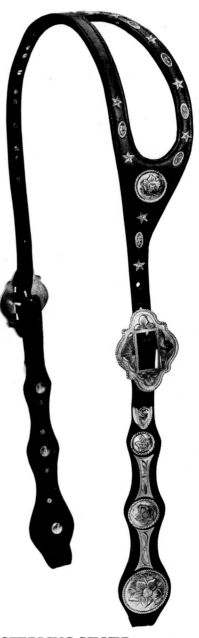

SIMCO's coordinated show outfit *(right)* has German silver trim with overlaid rope edge. Headstall, $172; breast strap, $170; matching reins, $56 pair.

TEX TAN's burgundy show halter *(far right)* features sterling silver mountings and white buckstitch trim. Matching lead strap comes with 18″ chain. $245.

ELABORATE SHOW BITS *(opposite)* with two exceptions* are stainless steel with sterling silver mountings. The exceptions are blue iron inlaid with sterling.

STERLING SILVER accents Ryon Saddlery's shaped-ear headstall. The ear loop has alternating stars and dots; the cheeks have rope-edged conchas. $350.

119

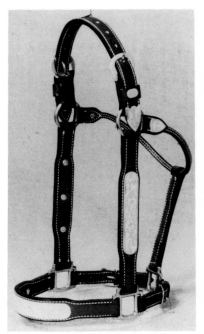

CUSTOM show halter by Tom Taylor features sterling silver plates overlaid with sterling scrolls. Price on request.

STERLING SILVER buckles and bars with rope-edged conchas highlight this halter from Ryon Saddlery. $325.

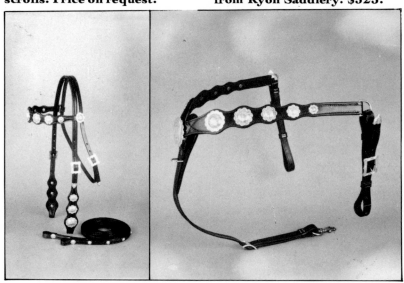

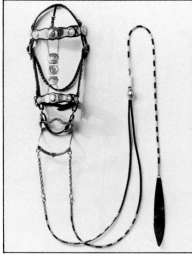

TEX TAN's scalloped leather show set is decorated with sterling silver buckle sets and graduated conchas. Headstall and reins (*left*), $485; breast strap (*right*), $450.

HAND-ENGRAVED sterling mounted breastplate (*above*) and bridle (*left*) were made by Edward Bohlin to match the silver show saddle on page 37. The breastplate, with its nine hangers and graduated silver conchas, weighs over ten pounds. Silver mountings are also used on the bridle. The bridle reins and romal are mounted with silver ferrules, and a large piece of decorative silver marks the point where they meet. The complete outfit is on display at H. Kauffman & Sons, New York City.

120

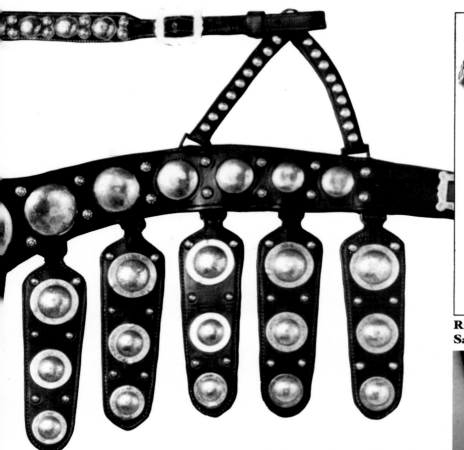

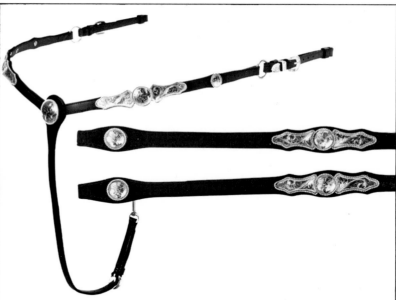

ROPE-EDGED sterling plates and conchas accent Ryon Saddlery's breast harness *(left)*, $250; reins *(right)*, $100.

General Rules for Cleaning Tack*

Do not allow residues of soaps, polishes, cleansers, or conditioners to build up on your equipment. Make sure all materials used in cleaning are either completely rubbed into your tack or wiped off it.

Before you try any new product, check its ingredients, and do not use any products your horse may be allergic to.

When cleaning your tack, always do the best job you possibly can. If you do slipshod work or take shortcuts, you only endanger yourself.

Caution: Even well-cared-for tack wears out eventually. Before every ride, make sure you examine all your equipment for cracks, weak spots, and loose hardware. If you find any defective parts, replace them immediately.

*From *Kauffman's Manual of Riding Safety*, by Sandra Kauffman, Clarkson N. Potter, 1977.

VOGT's hand-engraved sterling silver breast collars and headstalls are designed to your order with your choice of buckles, conchas, and plates. Collar *(left)*, $350; headstall *(right)*, $530.

121

TEXAS TALK

I f you are a tenderfoot who is heading West, you had better dispense with Modern English Usage and pick up a copy of Texas Talk (sold right here). Westerners in general and cowboys in particular have their own special lingo and can turn a colorful phrase faster than you can say howdy. Because Westerners live so much of their lives outdoors, most of their expressions are based on natural phenomena. Some of them, however, derive from the local culture — "Take it away, Leon" (after the fiddler in a Texas band) is a good example — and from the titles of popular songs and hymns. (Don't be surprised if you're greeted at the door with "*If I knew you were comin' I'd have baked a cake*.")

It is a good idea to study your cowboy dictionary before venturing too deeply into the heart of Texas. When a good-looking feller or a real pretty lady sidles up to you and asks "*How ya' doin'?*" you will certainly want to make the proper retort. (It's "*Just fine*," even if your wife has just left you or your house is on fire.) You will also want to learn which folks to avoid (*bad men, rustlers, ornery critters*, and their ilk) and which local events to attend. (Invited to a *roundup*, you would accept *lickety-split*, but you would never ride a *bronc* when you were all *duded up*.) In the West linguistic ignorance is seldom bliss. Not knowing the difference between a no-account *gunman* and a law-abiding *gunslinger* can get you into a *heap a trouble*, and if you don't come *a runnin'* when *the cookie* says "*Durned if h'it ain't time for grub*," you might end up *just starvin' to death*. And *that's enough to make a preacher cuss!*

Words

Blue Norther, or Norther a great mass of cold air from the North or East. One of the weather phenomena of the Southwest: the sky suddenly becomes dark blue and the temperature can fall below freezing in just half an hour.

Boot Hill a burying ground for bad men. Since bad men were generally hanged, they were said to die "with their boots on" and any cemetery that held them was therefore *Boot Hill*. Good men never died with their boots on, since they died in bed of natural causes.

Brushpopper a southwestern cowboy (who "popped" runaway cattle out of the brush).

Cow town the railroad town where the cowboy delivered his herd.

Cowpuncher, cowpoke synonyms for cowboy; originally, a cowboy who punched or poked cows with a long pole when loading them into cattle cars.

Coyote a prairie wolf.

Dogie an orphaned calf.

Fly low to drive fast.

Get het up to get upset.

High expensive.

Hot oil stolen merchandise.

Hung-up to catch one's foot in a stirrup when thrown from a horse.

Larrupin' scrumptious, delicious.

Maverick an unbranded calf, a stray.

Meddlesome Mattie a snoop.

Muley a hornless cow.

Mustang any wild horse.

Near, or close tight, stingy.

Necktie social a hanging.

Night-hawk the wrangler's nighttime replacement.

Old boy any male over eighteen.

Outlaw a wild horse; also, a desperado.

Pearl diver dishwasher.

Proud happy, as in "I'm so proud to be here."

Remuda a trail outfit's collection of saddle horses. Includes each cowboy's string.

Road agent a bandit.

Scream a live wire, applied only to females, as in "she's a scream."

Shindig a cowboy dance.

Slim tall. And even if you are tall and rotund.

Solemn quiet; not a talker.

Sorry worthless, lazy.

String a collection of horses assigned to a cowboy in a trail outfit. A string usually consisted of seven to ten horses.

Waddie slang term for cowboy.

Wrangler the cowboy in charge of the remuda.

Your place where you live; never "your house."

Phrases

Absolutely edified thrilled.

Agitated as a June bug very upset.

Ah ha! San Antone! Oh boy! Wow!

Busy as a tick in a tar bucket real busy.

Crooked as a barrel of snakes dishonest.

Fat as a turkey buzzard obese.

Good Night Nurse! Good grief!

Grin like a possum eatin' (per)simmons smirk.

Ill as a hornet nasty, crabby.

I've been to three state fairs and a goat ropin' and I ain't never seen nothin' like that! highly unusual.

Mad as an old wet hen furious.

Mean as the Bad Man mean as the Devil.

Mink-eyed hussy a lady who is up to no good.

More _____ than Carter had oats! No one seems to know for sure why Westerners say "More _____ than Carter had oats" while the rest of the country says "More _____ than Carter had pills." The following explanations have been suggested: 1. Carter sold oats to Westerners and pills to the rest of us. 2. Westerners have strong livers and don't need pills; Easterners are lily-livered and do. 3. Westerners are easily confused and say "oats" when they mean "pills." 4. There were two Carters.

Naked as a Jaybird nude.

Our kind of people la crème de la crème.

Plum wore out tired.

Ran like a scalded pup ran very fast.

Red as a turkey gobbler's neck bright red.

Shiny as a June bug glistening.

Slick as owl grease slippery or conniving.

Sorry as a buzzard's guts describes something that has a bad odor.

Take it away, Leon! let's begin. Leon was the fiddler in Bob Wills and his Texas Playboys, and after introducing each musical number Wills would say this.

The devil's beating his wife with a frying pan a sun shower.

The sun's drawing water you can see the sun's rays through the clouds.

Tight as Dick's hatband drunk, or stingy. (No one knows who Dick was.)

You talk like a Yankee your accent is different from mine.

You're gonna have a lot of stars in your crown! heaven will repay you for such a good deed; the phrase comes from the title of a popular hymn and is another example of a song title turned into a conversational phrase.

Ugly as mud, or Ugly as a mud fence really ugly.

Well I swan! My goodness!

Geographical Terms

New York an important town. You may not want to live there but a visit adds to your prestige.

Out West any place west of El Paso.

Up North everywhere but "Out West" or "New York."

OUTERWEAR

The cowboy's cold-weather wardrobe differs from yours and mine in one important respect: It does not contain an overcoat. To cope with the cruelties of the Western winter (and 60 degrees below zero is as cruel as you can get), a cowboy may wear a jacket, a slicker, or a vest, but the warmth and luxury of a full-length overcoat is denied him. The reason? Safety. The average overcoat is a heavy cumbersome garment that constricts the body and reduces its mobility. Since mobility is the cowboy's stock in trade and his life depends on an ability to move freely, quickly, and painlessly, he is forced to sacrifice warmth for security.

The cowboy's outerwear problems are not unfamiliar to other horsemen. Throughout history riders have longed for a winter habit that would give them freedom without also giving them pneumonia. Medieval knights thought they had the problem solved when they came up with the jerkin, a short (hip-length), sleeveless, leather coat that was thick enough to be worn as armor or as padding under mail. The jerkin kept out the cold, repelled the lance, and left the rider's arms free for jousting, plundering, and warring. Eventually, it evolved into an even shorter garment called a vest.

Vests were popular on the northern ranges for three reasons: They were warm, they were versatile, they were available. Made of leather or heavy cloth, they laced or buttoned down the front, and could be gussied up with beads and feathers and fancy stitching. They also had something the cowboy needed badly: pockets — places to store cigarette papers, tobacco, matches, and small objects.

Despite the popularity of the vest, not all Western outerwear was sleeveless. Cowboys often wore blanket-lined wool jackets to protect them from the frost, and in brush country they wore leather or canvas jackets (bush jackets) to keep the thorns from penetrating their skin. On the southern ranges, where the climate was fairly mild, a man could get through the winter in a hip-length woolen coat, but send him North and he would strap a great, big yellow slicker to the back of his saddle. This oiled-canvas "fish" was an all-weather coat, which meant that it made the cowboy equally uncomfortable in heat, cold, rain, or snow. Today's goosedown jackets are certainly an improvement. Loose, lightweight, and water-repellent, they are comfortable both in the saddle and out, and from the way they are selling in the West, it seems as if the cowboy's outerwear problem has finally been solved.

THROUGH THE AGES horsemen have sought winter garments that provide freedom of movement as well as warmth.

124

LEE's machine-washable denim vest has inset pockets, button front. Sheplers. $17.

YOKED COWHIDE vest with bellows pockets. Altman Western Leathers. $78.

LEE'S DENIM VEST has a polyester pile lining, side-entry pockets. Sheplers. $25.

MAHOPA'S FRINGED vest is white deer-skin with snail buttons. Billy Martin's. $410.

CHOCOLATE BROWN split cowhide vest from Schott Brothers boasts three rows of fringe, two pockets on a snap front. $70.

SCULLY'S FIVE-BUTTON glazed lamb vest features four rows of boot stitching on its yoke, inset pockets. At Cutter Bill's. $130.

WINCHESTER VEST by Char Designs comes in rich chocolate leather and features welted pockets, nickel buttons. $98.

127

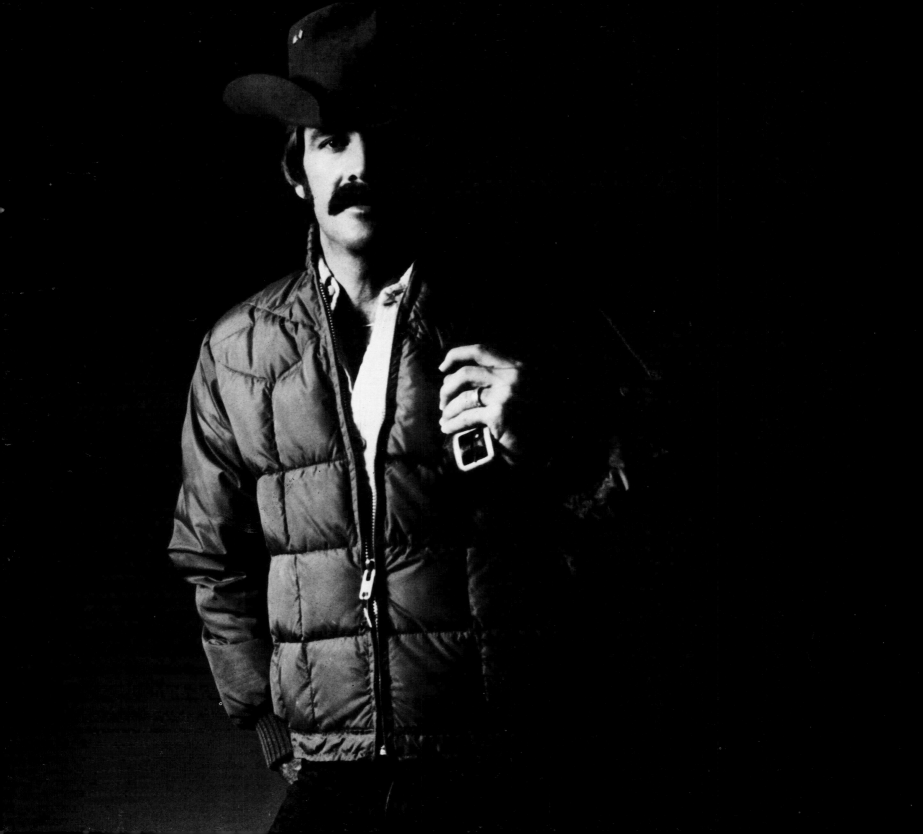

GOOSEDOWN vest is water-repellent nylon. Comfy. $60.

GERRY'S DOWN-FILLED nylon vest features suede cloth yoke, fleece-lined suede cloth pockets. H. Kauffman & Sons. $80.

ALL-DOWN parka by Gerry has suede cloth collar. $95.

GERRY'S DOWN-FILLED nylon parka (opposite) comes with an elasticized waistband and is reinforced at all stress points. $84.

NYLON SHELL of Comfy's goosedown vest is set off by contrasting piped yoke and pocket trim. $60.

GOOSEDOWN parka by Comfy has a pile collar with Velcro fastener, two-way pockets, knit cuffs, three-layer sleeves. $105.

129

PILE-LINED plaid work jacket from Trego's Westwear. $95.

TREGO'S TOPCOAT has a pile collar and lining. $100.

YOKED DENIM duster *(left)* is vented in the back to promote freedom of movement in the saddle. H. Kauffman & Sons. $150.

HIP-LENGTH SHEARLING jacket from Bert Paley Ltd. features roll-back cuffs, side pockets, roll-up collar. $300.

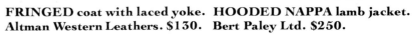

FULL-LENGTH yellow rubber rain slicker will protect both rider and saddle. Button closings at the ankles turn the vented skirt into leg coverings. H. Kauffman & Sons. **$45.**

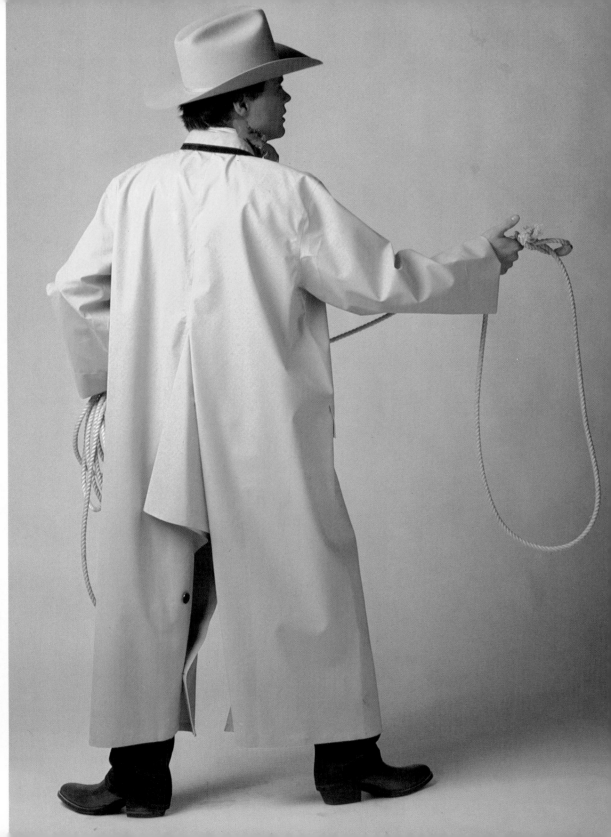

CHANNEL-QUILTED nylon vest with possum collar. Neiman-Marcus. $195.

QUILTED MONTANA VEST from Char Designs is made of chocolate leather and features natural American coyote collar, old buffalo nickel button closings. $470.

MAHOPA's deerskin jacket is accented by Winnebago bone. Billy Martin's. $925.

HALF-DOLLAR conchas spark Cutter Bill's hand-painted buffalo coat. $1,700.

FRINGED gold elk Chieftain by Mahopa has hair-pipe trim. Billy Martin's. $900.

133

SHIRTS

Remember when you played "Cowboys and Indians"? When you read Zane Grey and Frank Dobie, and followed the hero from Republic Studios to Television City? Remember when you dreamed of owning a real cowboy shirt, a white satin dazzler with red appliquéd roses and mile-long fringe? Well, pardner, I have sad news for you. If the old-time cowboy had offered you the shirt off his back, you would have refused it. What's more, you would have taken one look at it and canceled your subscription to *Western Life* magazine.

In the early days of the West, the cowboy shirt, with its dreary colors, dismal fabrics, and primitive styling, was not such stuff as either dreams or legends are made of. Good dyes were scarce and colors were limited to basic black, basic brown, basic gray, and basic blue. With few exceptions, winter shirts were wool, summer shirts were cotton. Pockets were rare, and collars so homely and poorly sewn that they were quickly concealed beneath bright southern bandannas. Only one bit of design was distinctive enough to outlive its time: the bib front. The bib was an additional layer of fabric that buttoned onto the shirt and its purpose was twofold: to provide extra warmth and to protect the cowboy from a bull's horns.

Despite his colorful reputation, the early cowboy was a conservative fellow and definitely not a fashion plate. He worked twelve to sixteen hours a day, had few social engagements, and was unlikely to dress for dinner. It was not until the Wild West Show and the rodeo that he developed a sense of style. Suddenly this retiring ranch hand was up onstage and out in the arena fighting bulls and broncs and Indians, and garnering wild applause. The applause put his life and his work in a new perspective. Riding, roping, and shooting were no longer a matter of life or death: They were show business and the cowboy was a star. In order to dress the part, he began borrowing bright colors and exotic patterns from the Mexican vaqueros, and fringes and beads from the Plains Indians. The result was the outrageously gaudy, wildly exuberant garment known as the cowboy shirt, and it was vivid proof that the ugly duckling of the Plains had turned into a dazzling swan.

BABY LAMB SUEDE shirts by Char Designs. His with toast piping, $268; hers with lightning flash yoke, $210.

SATIN SHIRTS for the King of the Cowboys and his girl. Prior's Larry Mahan Collection. $40.

COWGIRL SHIRT has piped yoke. H Bar C. $30.

RYON'S EQUITATION blouse with reversible bib. $75.

EMBROIDERED satin shirt. Cutter Bill. $40.

FROM LEFT to right: Handler-Fenton fringed lace-up shirt, $30; long-sleeved black cotton T-shirt with Cutter Bill's logo in silver glitter dust, $20; black His and Hers shirts striped with gold lurex, $38; Handler-Fenton piped shirt with embroidered appliqués, $38. Cutter Bill.

THE WESTERN SHIRT

The Western shirt is designed to meet the special needs of the working cowboy. The broad shoulders absorb the stress of riding and roping, and the tapered body prevents excess fabric from catching on the horns of a steer. The shoulders are reinforced with a yoke made from two layers of fabric, and this extra thickness gives the cowboy added protection against the steer's horns and the sun's rays. The front of the yoke generally comes to a point over each breast pocket. The back of the yoke (in the back of the shirt) may end in one, two, or three points.

There are two types of shirt pockets: half-moon, or smile, pockets and flap pockets. The half-moons are reinforced at the edges with stitched arrows; the flaps generally imitate the design of the yoke and are kept closed with a single snap.

The shirt closes with snaps rather than with buttons so that it can pop open if a horn gets caught beneath it. Wide cuffs ensure a snug fit at the wrists and make sure the sleeves do not crawl down the cowboy's hands and interfere with his roping.

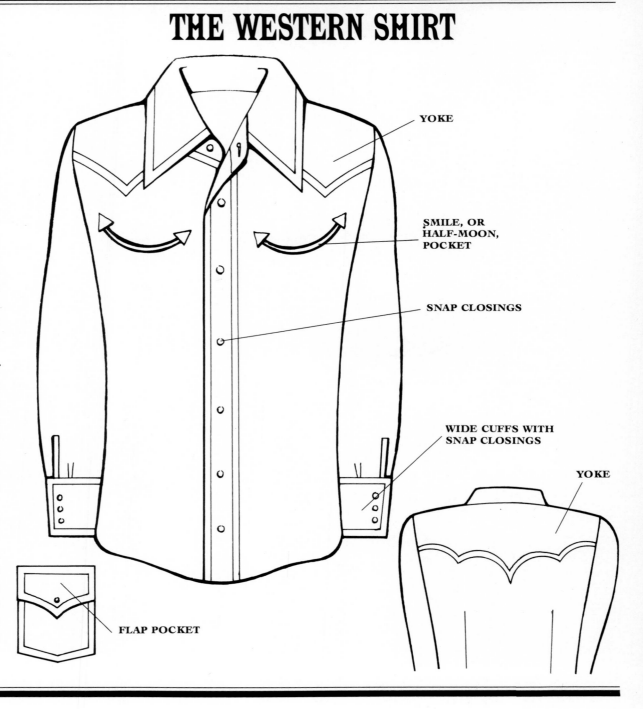

YOKE

SMILE, OR HALF-MOON, POCKET

SNAP CLOSINGS

WIDE CUFFS WITH SNAP CLOSINGS

YOKE

FLAP POCKET

NIGHT SHIRT by Karman is polyester/cotton and features unusual multicolored yoke. His and Hers, $24 each.

VAN HEUSEN's cotton plaid Baracuta features piped cape yoke, new short button-down collar, trimmed cuffs. $25.

FENTON WESTERNS' shirt with pointed yokes, collar, button-down pockets. $27.

DICKSON-JENKINS' plaid shirt has white piping on yoke, collar, cuffs. $30.

PLAID EQUITATION blouse with double-piped back yoke, solid cuffs. Ryon Saddlery. $75.

MILLER WESTERN WEAR's solid-colored shirt has print pocket flaps, piping, yoke. $25.

CHAPPARAL BY CHAMPION Western Wear is available in bright, solid colors with complementary plaid yokes and cuffs. A cotton and polyester Perma-press shirt, it has yoke-enclosed pockets, five mother-of-pearl snaps on each cuff. $20.

140

RODEO favorite Barry Burke in a Wrangler plaid. $20.

WRANGLER plaid, snared by Tom Ferguson. $20.

CHAMPION Leo Camarillo wears a Wrangler Western. $20.

MULTICOLORED STRIPES from H Bar C. $30.

STRIPES, LEAVES, and flowers enliven Karman's rodeo shirt. Pocket flaps repeat the design of the shoulder yoke. $20.

CHAMBRAY work shirt with snap closings. Wrangler. $20.

141

LARRY MAHAN *(top)*, rodeo's all-time All-Around Champion, wears a combination solid and print bib-front shirt with matching snaps. The lady's shirt features a similar, shorter bib. Larry Mahan Collection by Prior. $40 each.

BIB-FRONT frontier shirt *(left)* in almond baby lamb suede has toast lining, old buffalo nickel buttons. Char Designs. $290.

HANDLER-FENTON's twenty-button bib-front shirt *(right)* is tan acrylic with navy piping, plaid-lined cuffs. Cutter Bill. $40.

BIB-FRONT shirt from Prior's Mahan Collection. $40.

H BAR C's lively yoked shirt has a stitched, Mexican-style design, smile pockets. $40.

SWIRLING STITCHERY enhances this Miller Western Wear shirt. $25.

PIPED BIB-FRONT shirt from Miller Western Wear. $40.

FLOWERS on H Bar C's shirt are outlined with several rows of decorative stitching. $40.

KARMAN'S TWO-TONE shirt has embroidered floral yoke. Cutter Bill. $38.

COWBOY COOKBOOK

During the long and lonely cattle drives, the heart of every trail outfit was a horse-drawn kitchen on wheels called a "chuck wagon." Equipped with pots, pans, and cooking utensils, with Dutch ovens, tin dishes, and iron cutlery, the wagon carried a month's supply of provisions and was driven by the most important man in the outfit, the cook, or "cookie." More often than not, cookie was a retired cowhand and master magician who could turn staples like bacon, soda, salt pork, flour, cornmeal, tomatoes, onions, and beans into delectable chuck. Here are three of his most famous recipes.

SON OF A GUN STEW

Extract the heart, liver, pancreas, brains, kidneys, and marrow gut from a freshly killed steer. Wash thoroughly. Cut into small cubes, then place in a Dutch oven. Add 2 tablespoons suet and water to cover. Sprinkle with salt, pepper, and/or chili powder. Boil for 45 minutes or until tender. Thicken with 2 tablespoons flour, and cook for another 45 minutes.

SOURDOUGH BISCUITS

Sourdough, a staple of the Southwest, is fermented dough. The original batter is called a "starter," and whenever the dough is used for baking, part of the starter is set aside and then replenished with fresh flour and water. Renewed in this way, the dough can keep working for months, or even years.

To make your starter, add ½ cake yeast to ½ cup warm water. When the yeast has softened, add to the mixture ½ cup warm water, 1 teaspoon sugar, and 1¼ cups flour. (The dough must be good and thick. If it isn't, add more flour until the right consistency is reached.) Place the dough in a stone jar or in an enamel pot, cover tightly, and let stand in a warm place—in the sun or near a fire—for 24 hours. The warmth will keep the dough fermenting, and bubbles will start to form. The next day, add another cup of warm water, 1 teaspoon sugar, and enough flour to thicken. Again, cover tightly and let stand in a warm place until the dough is full of bubbles and has a good, sour smell. This should take 1 to 3 days.

To make the biscuits, pour part of the starter into a mixing bowl, add ½ teaspoon baking soda and a sprinkling of salt. Thicken with flour and knead thoroughly. Break the dough into biscuit-sized pieces, cover the tops with fat, and bake in a Dutch oven. When the biscuits are finished, replenish the starter by adding flour and warm water to the dough in the original jar. In this way there will always be an ample supply of dough on hand for bread, biscuits, and flapjacks.

COWBOY COFFEE

Add 1 pound coffee to 1 gallon water. Boil over a hot fire for 30 minutes. Pitch a horseshoe into the pot. If it sinks, add more coffee.

For the modern, well-heeled cowboy, the cookie is apt to be the chef at the best hostelry in town. And here are some of *his* recipes.

CANADIAN CHEESE SOUP

½ pound Velveeta cheese
1 to 1½ cups milk
1 pint half 'n half
½ cup onions
½ cup carrots
½ cup celery
4 tablespoons butter
2 tablespoons flour
2 cups chicken broth

Combine cheese, milk, and half 'n half in a double boiler, allow cheese to melt, then set mixture aside. Sauté onions, carrots, and celery in butter. Add flour and continue cooking for 1 minute, stirring continually to avoid sticking. Add the chicken broth and bring to a simmer. Add the milk and cheese mixture to the stock and simmer again. The soup should have a creamy texture. Serves 4.

From the Driskill Hotel, Austin, Texas

MENGER HOTEL SPINACH PUDDING

3 cups cooked spinach
½ small onion
½ green pepper
1½ garlic buds
4 eggs
1 teaspoon salt
¼ teaspoon pepper
dash of nutmeg
2 cups fine bread crumbs
½ cup softened butter

Put spinach, onion, green pepper, and garlic through food processor or grinder, using fine blade. Add eggs and seasonings, mixing well. Mix in 1½ cups of the crumbs. Take a clean dish towel and spread the butter onto it, forming a 9-to-10-inch square. Sprinkle with remaining bread crumbs. Drop spinach mixture in center and form into a roll about 1½ inches thick. Wrap cloth loosely around roll. Tie ends and middle securely with string. Steam 20 minutes. Serves 10 to 12.

From the Menger Hotel, San Antonio, Texas

TOURNEDOS CHANTARELLE

1 slice bread (4 to 7 ounces per serving)
2-to-3½-ounce beef tenderloin steak per serving
oil
parsley

CHANTARELLE SAUCE
½ cup cut green onions
1 cup dry chantarelles (drained, juice reserved)
butter
1 cup red wine
½ cup diced tomatoes
2 cups brown sauce
salt
pepper
Worcestershire sauce

Sauté green onions and dry chantarelles in small amount of butter, add red wine and diced tomatoes, and let cook until liquid is reduced by half. (Also reduce chantarelle juice.) Stir in brown sauce and cook 15 to 20 minutes more, then add salt, pepper, and Worcestershire sauce to taste.

Toast slice of bread, cut in half, and round corners.

Sauté tournedos in pan with small amount of oil, set steaks on toast, cover with sauce, and serve. Garnish with parsley if desired.

From the Shamrock Hilton, Houston, Texas

NINFA'S FRIED PORK

1 pork butt or butt end of pork loin, about 1½ pounds
3 tablespoons flour
¼ teaspoon salt
¼ teaspoon freshly ground black pepper
¼ teaspoon paprika
1 cup lard

Cut pork into 1-inch cubes or smaller. Discard fatty pieces. Mix flour, salt, pep-per, and paprika, and coat meat with all the mixture.

In a heavy skillet, heat lard over high heat until smoking. Carefully add pork, piece by piece, so lard will not splatter. Turn meat frequently so it browns evenly. It will take 4 to 5 minutes.

Remove meat to several layers of absorbent paper, cover with more paper, and pat dry. Transfer to a serving dish decorated with lettuce leaves. Serve with bowls of thick sour cream and hot avocado sauce. As a main course, serve with warmed buttered tortillas.

AVOCADO HOT SAUCE

1 ripe avocado
¼ cup sour cream
¼ cup milk
1 teaspoon minced onion
1 clove garlic, mashed with ¼ teaspoon salt
1 tablespoon minced fresh cilantro or ¼ teaspoon dried cilantro (parsley can be substituted)
½ teaspoon hot pepper sauce
2—3 tablespoons lemon juice

Peel avocado and mash. Add remaining ingredients and blend with a wire whisk. Let stand for at least an hour before serving.

From Ninfa's Restaurant, Houston, Texas

BELTS & BUCKLES

If you think the cowboy wore a belt to hold up his pants, you had better take another look at those pants. Skintight Levis need about as much holding up as the First Texas Bank.

In the early West only two types of belts were really important: those that supported the cowboy's back and those that supported his gun. Both were made of either calfskin or horsehide, and though they were often carved or decorated with metal disks called "conchas," they were basically protective devices.

The five-to-eight-inch-wide bronc-riding belt served as a brace. It was shaped to the cowboy's body and allowed him to break horses without also breaking his back. The holster, or cartridge, belt, a two-to-three-inch-wide miniature arsenal, carried the cowboy's gun and ammunition, and came in three different styles. The simplest held one pistol and a single row of cartridges, and rested loosely on the cowboy's hips so that the pistol could be easily drawn. The second held two types of cartridges to accommodate the Texas Rangers and others who packed both a six-shooter and a rifle. Made of two layers of leather, it had a slitted opening beneath the buckle and doubled as a money belt. Finally, there was the Buscadero, an elaborate two-pistol affair that was worn occasionally by lawmen and much more frequently by movie cowboys.

Eventually, when the West was no longer so wild, the belt began to lead a more peaceful, decorative life. It laid down its arms, crept up to the cowboy's waist, and became a showcase for silver buckles and hand-carved leather. Leather carving, a Moorish art that the Mexicans learned from the Spanish, had originally been employed in the decoration of saddles. Later, when belts too were carved, the traditional designs of leaves, flowers, and stems were maintained.

Today, the Western belt is an ornate accessory that can be fashioned from inexpensive cowhide or from exotic skins costing hundreds of dollars. No matter what it is made of, however, it is sure to be strong and unusually wide, just as it was in the old days when it carried the weight of the cowboy's gun.

IN THE early West the belt was a protective device. Today it is a setting for leather carving and elaborate silver buckles.

RYON SADDLERY's 1½″ hand-carved, hand-finished belts are made of top grain saddle leather and come with either a tan or mahogany background. *Top:* buckstitched with name, $26; *center:* with name, $24; *bottom:* buckstitched, $22. Prices do not include buckles.

148

FLORAL DESIGNS and matching buckles highlight Kon Kut's 1½″ to 2″ wide filigree "name" belts. Nocona Belt Co. $35.

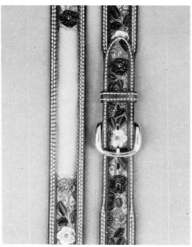

EMBOSSED with acorn and oak-leaf design, Tex Tan's belt has buckstitching and a 7″ nameplate. $25.

TEX TAN's 1¾″ embossed cowhide belt is accented with a floral motif and white saddle-stitched border. $22.

BUCKLES

Some men long for solid gold Cadillacs, Emerald Cities, and diamonds as big as the Ritz, but the cowboy's passion is silver. Silver bits. Silver spurs. Silver bands and tips and ties. And, especially, silver buckles. Buckles as big and as bright as prairie moons. Buckles that glow with bronzed horses and burnished calves, with jeweled flowers and sculpted vines. Buckles that darn near knock your eyes out!

Where did these jeweled and sculpted saucers come from and how did the cowboy get them? Given his environment, his neighbors, and the fabulous silver mines of the West, the cowboy's love of silver was almost inevitable. Surrounded by the Mexicans, who decorated their clothes and equipment with conchas and huge silver buttons, and the Navahos who adorned themselves and their bits, bridles, and headstalls with gleaming art, the cowboy grew up with the work of expert silversmiths. By the time he was ready to compete in horse shows and rodeos, he had learned how to use the lode around him. As a performer, a public person, a little flash was good for his image. It was also good for business. Audiences enjoyed the elaborate costumes and trappings as much as they enjoyed the riding and roping. And the cowboy enjoyed being a hero. How did he know he was a hero? Simple. For breeding the best horse or for roping a calf in the shortest possible time, he was awarded a Western-style laurel leaf, a trophy bearing all the details of his triumph: an enormous silver buckle.

Luckily, we ordinary folk do not have to go into the arena for a beautiful silver trophy. We just have to go into a saddlery shop and order one. That may not make us genuine heroes, but once we get those big gorgeous buckles on, who will be the wiser?

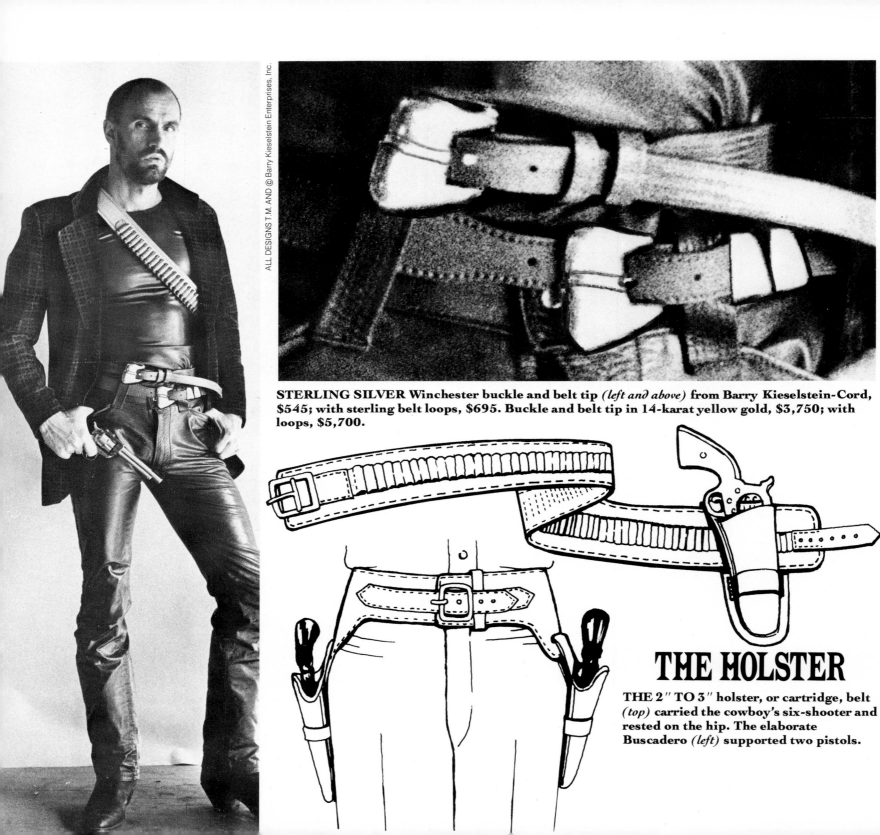

STERLING SILVER Winchester buckle and belt tip *(left and above)* from Barry Kieselstein-Cord, $545; with sterling belt loops, $695. Buckle and belt tip in 14-karat yellow gold, $3,750; with loops, $5,700.

THE HOLSTER

THE 2″ TO 3″ holster, or cartridge, belt *(top)* carried the cowboy's six-shooter and rested on the hip. The elaborate Buscadero *(left)* supported two pistols.

GERMAN SILVER concha belts in top grain cowhide. *Left:* $47; *center:* $32; *right:* with embossed floral design, $38. Nocona Belt.

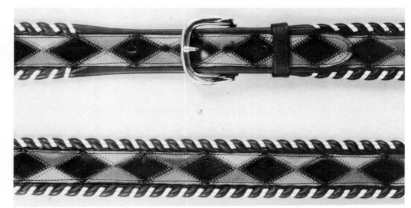

ALUMINUM-LACED patchwork belt. Tex Tan. $65. The buckle is not included in the price.

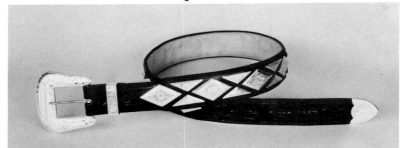

TEX TAN BELT with engraved sterling silver mountings and buckle set. $800.

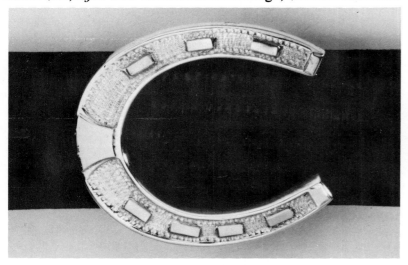

STERLING SILVER good luck buckle fits 1½″ belt. Ryon Saddlery. $30.

RYON SADDLERY's sterling buckle and tip is designed for chap belts. $32.

CUSTOM-MADE STERLING silver hand-engraved buckle set has 14-karat gold rope edge. Tom Taylor. Price on request.

SCULPTED sterling tip to fit 1½″ belt. Tom Taylor. $38.

STERLING tip, jeweler's bronze figure. Tom Taylor. $38.

STERLING SILVER ORIGINALS by Tom Taylor. *From top:* hand-engraved buckle set (buckle, loop, tip) with rope edge, $75. Buckle set with 14-karat gold initial on brown snake belt, and without initial on gray snake belt, prices on request. Havana brown English bridle leather belt with two-loop buckle set. Belt, $38; buckle set, $70; 1″ hazel snake belt with buckle set. Belt, $75; buckle set, $63. Blue snake handbag with custom hand-carved corners and fastener, $175; also available in hand-carved Havana brown English bridle leather *(not shown)*, $150.

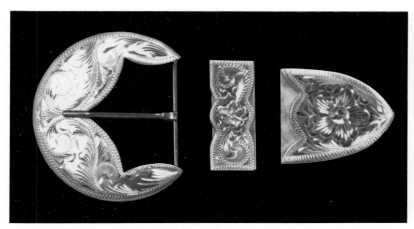

THREE-PIECE sterling buckle set for 1½″ belt. Vogt. $107.

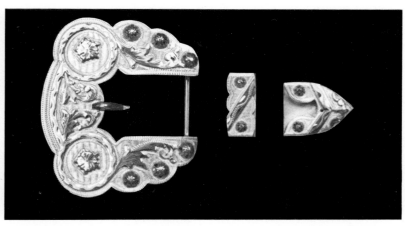

VOGT'S STERLING buckle set with 14-k gold overlay. $425.

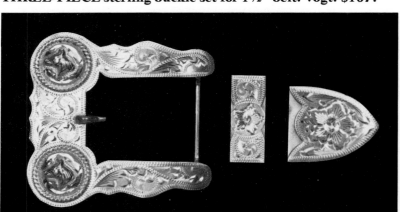

STERLING BUCKLE SET overlaid with 14-k gold. Vogt. $200.

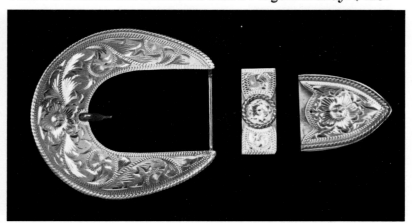

ENGRAVED sterling buckle set with rope edge. Vogt. $200.

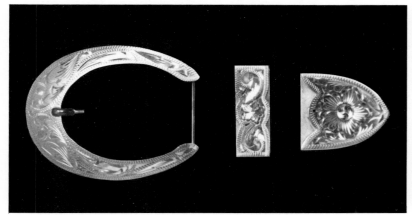

STERLING SILVER hand-engraved buckle set. Vogt. $140.

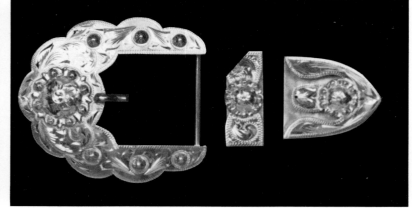

ENGRAVED sterling loop, tip, and scalloped buckle. Vogt. $187.

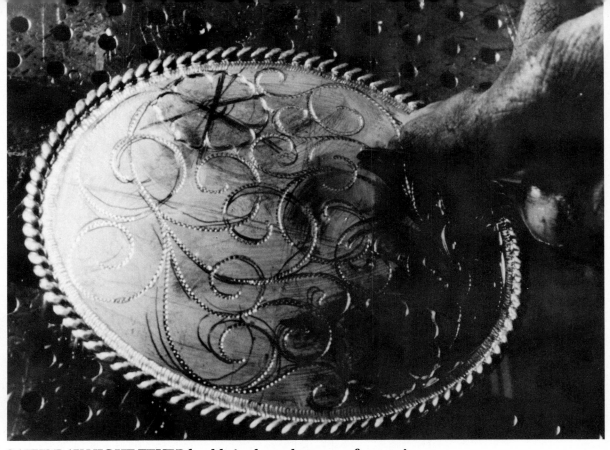

TOM TAYLOR and buckle.   **SATURDAY NIGHT FEVER buckle in the early stages of engraving.**

TAYLOR CUTS 14-karat gold filigree trim for trophy buckle overlay.

AFTER BEING SOLDERED to the buckle, the filigree work is polished.

154

CAST AND SOLDERED, these sterling silver rope-edged buckle sets and large trophy buckles are ready for engraving and polishing.

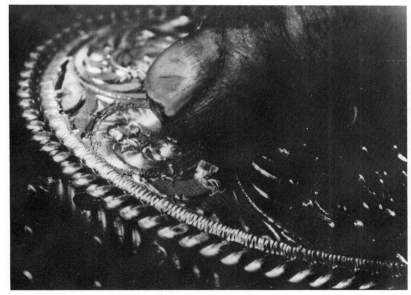

TAYLOR ADDS VEINING to a leaf design on the Saturday Night Fever buckle.

A SMALL RUBY is set into the center of a 14-karat gold engraved ornamental flower.

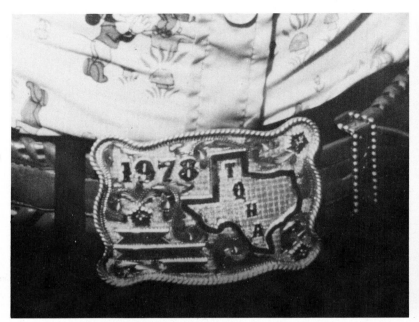

CHAMPIONSHIP TROPHY buckles inscribed with name, date, and place of competition. *Below:* cowgirls also win trophies.

BRONZE NAME BUCKLE, 4″ × 3″, is mounted with sterling letters and fits 1½″ belts. Six letter limit. Ryon Saddlery. $65.

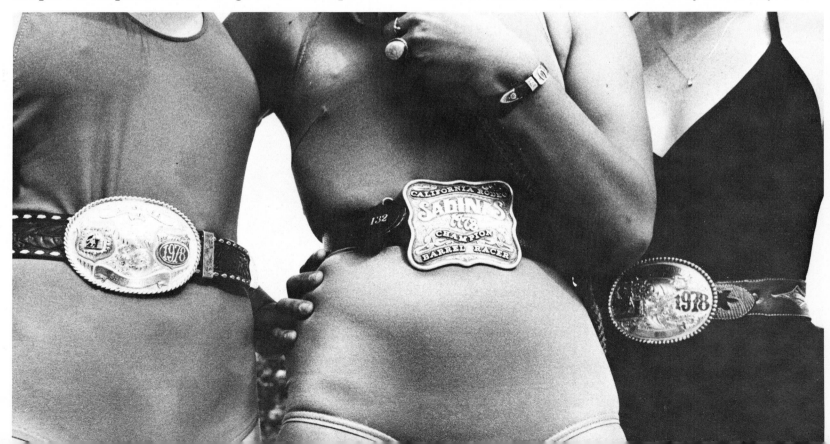

TOM TAYLOR. $1,200.

VOGT. $413.

TOM TAYLOR. $3,000.

VOGT. $350.

TOM TAYLOR. $3,000.

VOGT. $565.

VOGT. $382.

VOGT. $615.

VOGT. $367.

TOM TAYLOR. $2,500.

VOGT. $360.

TOM TAYLOR. $2,700.

THE COWBOY CODE

In all societies there are unwritten laws that good men live by. The cowboy's code of ethics was a simple one but each "law" was backed up by good, sound reasoning.

IT IS ill-mannered to ask any man his name. (It may be that for one reason or another he cannot afford to bring notice to himself.)

STEALING a man's horse is a crime punishable by death. (Leaving a man stranded on the Plains, miles from food, water, or shelter, is as good as killing him.)

CHEATING at cards is an unpardonable offense. (The victim or one of his friends is entitled to retaliate with a six-shooter.)

DRAWING a six-shooter on an unarmed man is strictly prohibited. (Offenders may be gunned down on the spot by the victim — if he is able — or by one of his friends.)

ENCOUNTERING a stranger on a trail, a man must approach him and speak a few words before moving off in another direction. (The greeting establishes his good intentions.)

WHEN TWO men meet, speak, and pass on, neither man must look back over his shoulder. (Such a look is an indication of distrust, a sign that the man doing the looking expects a shot in the back.)

WHEN GREETING a stranger on a trail, it is proper to nod and say "Howdy"; it is not proper to wave. (A raised hand may cause a skittish horse to bolt.)

WHEN A stranger dismounts to cool his horse, it is not polite to remain in the saddle while carrying on a conversation with him. (The proper thing to do is to dismount and speak to him face to face so he can see what you are up to.)

TO RIDE another man's horse without first asking his permission is a grave insult. (A horse is private property, and borrowing one without leave is equivalent to slapping his owner's face.)

ONLY IN dire emergency is it permissible to borrow a horse. (Every man has his own style of riding, and a horse can easily be spoiled by the wrong kind of rider.)

A SMART rider always puts his horse's comfort before his own. (If the horse becomes lame or disabled, the rider may find himself stranded in the middle of the desert.)

Trucks & Trailers

In the 1800s the cowboy was a veritable Jack-of-all-trades. In addition to tending cattle, he broke horses, dug ditches, cleared away brush, put up fences, cared for equipment, and, in general, did whatever was necessary to keep the ranch running smoothly. Today, the cowboy's job is not very different from what it was a hundred years ago; what *is* different is the manner in which it is performed. Where once the cowboy had only his hands and a horse to work with, he now has powerful machines that give him the speed, safety, and comfort his predecessors could only have dreamed of.

In the Old West, the cowboy's greatest asset was his horse; in the New West, it is his pickup or his jeep. Made to withstand the extremes of climate, these rugged, multipurpose vehicles can be driven over mountains, deserts, and brush country, and are admirably suited to difficult and demanding ranch work. The one-quarter-ton jeep, which was developed for reconnaissance missions in World War II, and was sturdy enough to tow trailers and airplanes, is remarkably adept at maneuvering in tight and dangerous situations. Thanks to its four-wheel drive, it has tremendous stability on slippery surfaces and bad roads (and places where there are no roads at all), and can keep moving as long as there is traction on any *one* of its wheels.

The pickup too is often available with four-wheel drive, and besides strength and durability it has the capacity to haul men, horses, cattle, and heavy equipment over long distances. What's more, it is designed to accommodate a slide-in camper, a definite attraction for the rodeo cowboy who spends months on the road, traveling from show to show.

In addition to their regular features, jeeps and pickups may be equipped with many invaluable extras: hole and trench diggers, snowplows, trailer tows, and even log splitters. And if the vehicle does happen to get stuck, there is always the electric winch, with eight thousand pounds of pull, to get it going again.

The modern cowboy may not have given up his horse completely, but there is no doubt that he is more often behind a wheel than atop a saddle. In fact, the pickup has become so much a part of his twentieth-century image that it is known affectionately as the "Cowboy Cadillac." And if we want any further proof of the extent to which jeeps and pickups have conquered the range, we have only to look at their names: Cheyenne, Renegade, Lariat, Round-Up.

PICKUPS, TRAILERS, and jeeps provide today's cowboy with the speed, safety, and comfort his predecessors could only have dreamed about.

PRICES SHOWN on the following pages for pickups, trailers, and jeeps are base prices for standard models. The cost of a vehicle will vary, depending on selected options.

WYOMING COWBOYS enjoy their multipurpose "Cadillac."

D50 SPORT from Dodge is a light-duty pickup truck with rear-wheel

FORD'S RANGER LARIAT with Tu-Tone exterior, twin I-beam front suspension. $5,399.

CHEVROLET'S EL CAMINO, a ligh

and a four-cylinder engine. $5,692.   HONCHO, AMC'S JEEP PICKUP, has four-wheel drive, cargo capacity of 77.7 cubic feet. $7,074.

y pickup, has optional V-eight engine, stereo cassette player. $5,591.   CHEVROLET's Wideside can accommodate a camper. $5,371.

FORD'S BRONCO is a four-wheeler with V-eight engine. $7,897.

DODGE'S RAMCHARGER has four-wheel drive. $8,198.

INTERNATIONAL HARVESTER's Scout II offers 82 cubic feet of car

AMERICAN MOTOR's CJ Renegade has four-wheel drive, three-speed transmission. $6,095.

pace, optional diesel engine. $7,748. CHEVROLET'S BLAZER, has power steering on all four-wheel drive models. $7,644.

165

TRAILERS

Back in the old days, before cars, trucks, and jeeps came along, it was the horse that transported the cowboy. Today the cowboy often transports his horse, and since both spend many hours on the road, the modern trailer must cater to the safety and comfort of each of them. The horse's needs are served by all-steel frames that prevent accidents by preventing the trailer joints from loosening, by high ceilings that cut down on head injuries, and by equalizers, which keep the vehicle level on rough roads and help the horse maintain his balance. Cowboys value the electric brake systems, which augment the hydraulic brakes, the easy loading platforms, the low centers of gravity, which keep the trailers hugging the road and make them easier to tow, and the interior lighting, which allows the driver to keep an eye on his horse while traveling at night. Today's trailers are also available with luxurious dressing rooms, and these not only come with carpeting and paneling, but with special doors that are designed to hold tack trunks.

Trailers are made in many different sizes and will accommodate two to eight horses. To pull a van that holds two horses, you will need approximately 200 horsepower or, at the very least, a medium-sized car with a V-eight engine. (A small foreign or compact car will not be strong enough to handle the load safely.) To pull four horses, you should have a one-half-ton pickup truck or a heavy-duty station wagon. A six- or eight-horse trailer requires a one-ton truck with heavy-duty radiator, transmission, differential, and suspension.

FOUR-HORSE gooseneck stock trailer from Johnston is 72″ wide, 84″ high, with four-wheel electric brakes. $2,950.

TWO-HORSE CLASSIC by Cherokee is 84″ high, 72″ wide, and features enclosed flyers and a front escape door. $3,250.

GENERAL TRAILER's four-horse Classic has independent suspension, allowing for three-tire towing in emergencies. $8,775.

SIX-HORSE Cherokee head-to-head trailer *(left)*, with side loading ramp *(right)*. $8,100.

CHEROKEE's two-horse gooseneck trailer with dressing room for small trucks. $4,300.

REAR VIEW of an early four-horse Hartman trailer shows loaded horses.

TWO-HORSE Deluxe Cherokee is 60″ wide, 78″ high. $2,400.

HARTMAN'S TWO-HORSE Pierce Arrow Deluxe has a 6′ long carpeted and paneled dressing room and all-steel frame. $6,175.

167

THE RODEO

Every February cowboys from all over the country gather in Texas to lock horns with the meanest, wildest, buckingest critters on four legs. The gathering is known as the Annual Houston Livestock Show and Rodeo, and last year approximately 900,000 people from twenty-nine countries jammed the Astrodome to watch it. By the time the show was over, the judges had awarded the contestants more than $200,000 in prize money, and hundreds of thousands of dollars had been spent on parades, bands, barbecues, trophies, and scholarships to agricultural schools.

The Houston Rodeo is one of the richest and biggest shows of its kind in the world. But for the professional cowboy, whose sole support is his prize money, it is just one more stop on the circuit, one show out of the many hundreds that are held annually in the United States and Canada. For rodeo today is big business, where danger, excitement, pageantry, and tradition are combined into one of the world's most popular spectator sports.

Just what is a rodeo? The word — pronounced "roh-dee-oh," not "roh-day-oh" — is Spanish for roundup. Traditionally, when roundup was over, cowboys from different cattle outfits would compete in contests of skill, trying to outdo one another in the three Rs: ridin', ropin', 'n 'restlin'. In 1883 these contests were presented to the general public for the first time. Their success was instantaneous, and by 1929, when the first cowboy's association was formed, rodeo was no longer an informal, impromptu event but a strictly monitored sport. Today, the Professional Rodeo Cowboys Association, a group run by and for cowboys, makes the rules for all contests and determines the type of equipment riders will use. The rules are designed to protect both cowboys and livestock, and to make sure that all contestants have an equal chance of winning. The cowboy pays a fee for each event that he enters and that fee entitles him to compete for the prize money. How much prize money? Surprisingly little. According to the PRCA, there are just one hundred professional cowboys who take home more than ten thousand dollars a year. The rest take home little more than their dreams and a fierce determination to do better the next time around.

THE COMBINATION of danger, excitement, pageantry, and tradition has made rodeo one of the world's most popular spectator sports.

The Top 27 Rodeos in the United States and Canada

The rodeos listed below are those that offer the highest purses to competing cowboys. Contestants must be members of the Professional Rodeo Cowboys Association.

ALBUQUERQUE, N. MEX.
New Mexico State Fair
mid-September

CALGARY, ALTA., CAN.
Exhibition and Stampede
early July

CHEYENNE, WYO.
Frontier Days Rodeo
late July

DALLAS, TEX.
State Fair of Texas
early October

DENVER, COLO.
National Western Rodeo
mid-January

EDMONTON, ALTA., CAN.
Canadian Western Super
late March

ELLENSBURG, WASH.
Ellensburg Rodeo
early September

FORT WORTH, TEX.
Southwest Exposition and
Fat Stock Show Rodeo
late January

HOUSTON, TEX.
Livestock Show and
Rodeo
late February

LAS VEGAS, NEV.
Elks Helldorado Rodeo
late May

MONTREAL, QUE., CAN.
Rodeo Show Montreal
mid-August

NAMPA, IDAHO
Snake River Stampede
mid-July

OGDEN, UTAH
Pioneer Days Rodeo
mid-July

OKLAHOMA CITY, OKLA.
State Fair Championship
Rodeo
late September

OMAHA, NEBR.
Ak-Sar-Ben Livestock
Exposition and Rodeo
mid-September

PENDELTON, OREG.
Round Up Rodeo
mid-September

PHOENIX, ARIZ.
Jaycees Rodeo of Rodeos
mid-March

PUEBLO, COLO.
Colorado State Fair
Rodeo
late August

PUYALLUP, WASH.
Western Washington Fair
Rodeo
mid-September

SAINT PAUL, OREG.
early July

SALINAS, CALIF.
California Rodeo
mid-July

SALT LAKE CITY, UTAH
Days of '47 Rodeo
mid-July

SAN ANTONIO, TEX.
Livestock Exposition
Rodeo
mid-February

SAN FRANCISCO, CALIF.
Grand National Rodeo
late October

SIDNEY, IOWA
Iowa's Championship
Rodeo
early August

TUCSON, ARIZ.
La Fiesta de los Vaqueros
Rodeo
late February

WYOMING, MICH.
Great Lakes
Championship Rodeo
mid-July

RODEO EVENTS

The average rodeo is composed of seven or eight different events, all of which demand highly specialized skills. The events are divided into two categories: rough stock events and timed events. In a rough stock event, the cowboy rides a bucking horse or a bull for a specified length of time and is judged on his form and on his spurring ability. A timed event is judged on speed, and the winner is the man who gets the job done in the shortest possible time. Today competition is so keen that the contestants are usually divided by mere tenths of a second.

ROUGH STOCK EVENTS
Saddle Bronc Riding

This is the cornerstone of all rodeo competition and the rules are heavily weighted in the animal's favor. The cowboy, equipped with a regulation PRCA saddle and a single rein, must remain on the back of a wild, bucking bronc for eight seconds. He must apply his spurs to the horse's sides and shoulders, but must not allow his free hand to touch the animal or the equipment. If he is bucked off before the eight seconds are up, he is disqualified.

Saddle bronc riders protect their legs with light leather chaps, and their spurs must have short shanks and dull rowels so that the animal cannot be cut.

Bareback Bronc Riding

The youngest of the three stock events, bareback bronc riding grew up in the arena and is not related to any type of ranch work. It is similar to saddle bronc riding except that, here, the rider sits on a bareback rigging instead of on a saddle. The rigging is a thick leather pad that is cinched to the horse's back. It has no stirrups or reins — only a leather handhold — and, again, the rider must not allow his free hand to touch the animal or the equipment.

In addition to spurs and chaps, bareback riders wear tough leather gloves to protect their hands.

Bull Riding

The speed and power of the two-thousand-pound Brahma bull make this the most difficult and dangerous of all rodeo events. The rider, who risks being trampled and gored, supports himself by holding onto a braided manila rope that is looped around the bull's belly. His free hand cannot touch the bull at any time and he must remain mounted for eight seconds. He is not required to spur the animal, but may receive extra credit if he does. When he dismounts, or is thrown, bull-baiting clowns enable him to make a safe getaway. A rider who is in the air or on the ground when the eight-second buzzer sounds is disqualified.

Bull riders protect themselves with chaps, spurs, and gloves.

TIMED EVENTS
Calf Roping

This event demands perfect teamwork between the cowboy and his horse. The cowboy, equipped with two twenty-five-foot lariats and a slim six-foot rope called a "piggin' string," is required to ride after the

calf and rope it. If he succeeds (he is allowed only two throws of the lariat), his horse immediately begins to back up, keeping the rope taut so that the calf cannot squirm out of it. The cowboy then dismounts, throws the calf to the ground, and ties three of its legs together with the piggin' string. When the tying is completed, he signals for time by releasing the string, and the judge approves the tie.

Calf ropers are allowed to select their own saddles and bridles, and though they may choose any type of mount, the fast and powerful Quarter Horse is their particular favorite.

Steer Wrestling

Also known as "bulldogging," steer wrestling is not a product of the ranch but of the Wild West Show, where it is supposed to have been invented by a black cowboy star named Bill Pickett. Pickett threw steers as easily as some men throw baseballs, and in this event the contestant must leap from a running horse onto a steer's back, grab the steer's horns, and wrestle the animal to the ground, making sure that it lies flat on its side, with its head and feet pointing in the same direction.

The steer wrestler requires no special equipment, but is assisted by a "hazer," another mounted cowboy who tries to keep the steer on a straight course.

Team Roping

In this event, two mounted cowboys team up to rope a steer. The "header" ropes the animal's horns, the "heeler" ropes its hind legs. When the job is done, both men wrap, or "dally," their ropes around the horns of their saddles and stand facing each other on horseback, the steer between them. The ropers are allowed a total of three throws, and may choose their own saddles and bridles. Roping saddles generally have a high horn to make dallying easier.

Steer Roping

Armed with an unbreakable nylon lariat, the mounted cowboy snares the horns of a running steer and lays the rope's slack over the animal's right hip. As the rope tightens, he angles his horse to the left and spins the steer to the ground. The horse then leans into the rope, keeping the steer prone so that the rider can dismount and tie it.

The roper uses his own saddle and bridle and is allowed only two throws of the lariat. He can tie together any three of the steer's legs. However, to tie a Brahma bull singlehandedly is so difficult that only about a dozen rodeos still feature this type of roping.

Cowgirl's Barrel Racing

A special event open only to women. The cowgirl races her horse around three large barrels that are set up in a triangular pattern. If she knocks over a barrel, several seconds are added to her time.

DRAWSTRING BAG holds 1¼ pounds rosin. Tex Tan. $4.75.

NINETEEN-STRAND mohair cincha by Bob Blackwood has four crossbars, steel "D" ring. $12.50.

HEAVY-DUTY bullrope bag. Bob Blackwood. $16.90.

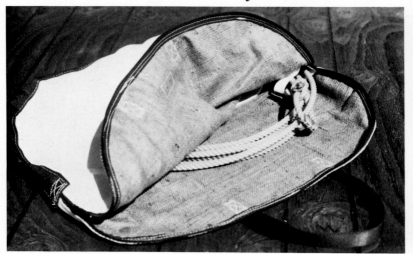

COTTON CANVAS rope bag with burlap insulation by Leo Camarillo can be soaked to prevent heat damage to ropes. $24.95.

CHAMPION ROPER Leo Camarillo and tools.

COLORFUL Tex Tan bag with 1 pound black rosin. $5.50.

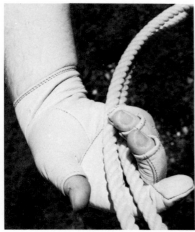

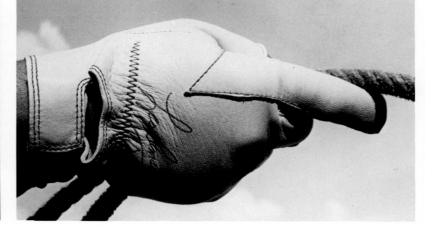

CAMARILLO goathide roping glove with reinforced palm. Open fingertips allow contestant to "feel the rope." $16.

WHITE DUCK carryall with protective blanket lining. Tex Tan. $20.50.

HEAVY-DUTY gear bag. Bob Blackwood. Small, $37.50; large, $45.

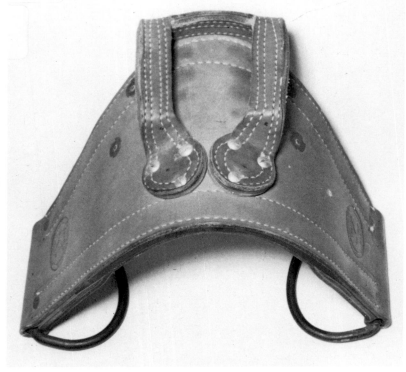

BULL ROPE has leather-plaited handhold. Tex Tan. $36.50.

DOUBLED LATIGO leather halter. Bob Blackwood. $50.

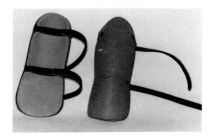

BOB BLACKWOOD rigging with rawhide handhold. $135.

GIRLS' BAREBACK rigging has a leather body, Neolite core, and leather/rawhide double handhold. Bob Blackwood. $97.50.

BARREL RACER's shin guards. Bob Blackwood. $40.80.

177

RODEO CHAMPIONS

At the end of each year the Professional Rodeo Cowboys Association (PRCA) announces the names of the top money winners in each rodeo event. The seven cowboys and one cowgirl whose photographs and biographies appear here have won the 1978 World Championship titles in saddle bronc riding, bareback bronc riding, bull riding, calf roping, steer wrestling, team roping, and barrel racing. The most prestigious title—World All-Around Cowboy—was won for the fifth consecutive year by Tom Ferguson, who, in 1976, became the first pro-rodeo cowboy to earn $100,000 in a single season. (To date, Ferguson's winnings total over $500,000.) Should Ferguson capture the All-Around title once more, he will tie the record of rodeo's number one celebrity, Larry Mahan, who, despite his retirement, is still known as the King of the Cowboys.

BUTCH KIRBY

LYNN McKENZIE
Shreveport, Louisiana
World Champion Barrel Racer
Season's Earnings: $20,508
Years as a Pro: 2

BUTCH KIRBY
Alba, Texas
Champion Bull Rider
Born: 1955; Years as a Pro: 12
Championship Season
Earnings: $44,926
Career Arena Earnings:
$141,631

178

DAVE BROCK
Pueblo, Colorado
Champion Calf Roper
Born: 1951; Years as a Pro: 8
Championship Season
Earnings: $60,790
Career Arena Earnings:
$194,745

DAVE BROCK

TOM FERGUSON

TOM FERGUSON
Miami, Oklahoma
Champion All-Around Cowboy
World Champion Steer Wrestler
Born: 1950; Years as a Pro: 8
Championship Season
Earnings: $131,233
Career Arena Earnings:
$439,602

JOE MARVEL
Battle Mountain, Nevada
Champion Saddle Bronc Rider
Born: 1955; Years as a Pro: 7
Championship Season
Earnings: $61,400
Career Arena Earnings:
$117,732

JOE MARVEL

JACK WARD

JACK WARD
Springdale, Arkansas
Champion Bareback Rider
Born: 1948; Years as a Pro: 11
Championship Season
Earnings: $55,183
Career Arena Earnings:
$242,792

BRAD SMITH
Prescott, Arizona
Champion Team Roper
Born: 1952; Years as a Pro: 6
Championship Season
Earnings: $29,467
Career Arena Earnings:
$32,974

GEORGE RICHARDS
Humboldt, Arizona
Champion Team Roper
Born: 1957; Years as a Pro: 4
Championship Season
Earnings: $20,555
Career Arena Earnings:
$31,911

BRAD SMITH AND GEORGE RICHARDS

DEBBIE JOHNSTON
Fort Worth, Texas
"Miss Rodeo America, 1979"
Born: November 19, 1954

LARRY MAHAN

LARRY MAHAN
Dallas, Texas
"Rodeo Man of the Year"
Born: 1943; Years as a Pro: 16
Career Arena Earnings:
$506,841

181

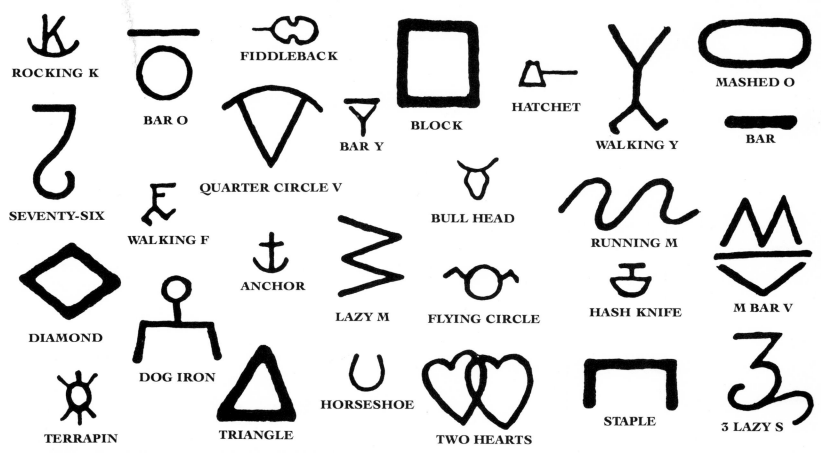

ROCKING K

BAR O

FIDDLEBACK

BLOCK

HATCHET

MASHED O

BAR Y

WALKING Y

BAR

SEVENTY-SIX

QUARTER CIRCLE V

WALKING F

BULL HEAD

RUNNING M

DIAMOND

ANCHOR

LAZY M

FLYING CIRCLE

HASH KNIFE

M BAR V

TERRAPIN

DOG IRON

TRIANGLE

HORSESHOE

TWO HEARTS

STAPLE

3 LAZY S

HORSE & CATTLE BRANDS

In the Old West it was customary for horses and cows from different ranches to graze together on the open range. To make sure each animal was returned to its rightful owner, an identifying mark called a "brand" was burned onto its skin with a hot iron. The brand, which was the owner's trademark, was made up of simple pictures, letters, numbers, and geometric shapes. However, the positioning of a brand was as important as the symbol or symbols that composed it. For example, two cattlemen might use the letter "D," but as long as one branded it on an animal's neck and the other on a shoulder, there would be no confusion of ownership. Also, the letter "D" could be read several different ways. Standing upright, it was read as "Big D." Lying on its side, it became "Lazy D." Enclosed in a circle, it was "Circle D."

Brands were either stamped on the animal's hide with a "stamping iron," or written on with a "running iron," a metal rod that was used like a pencil. In de-

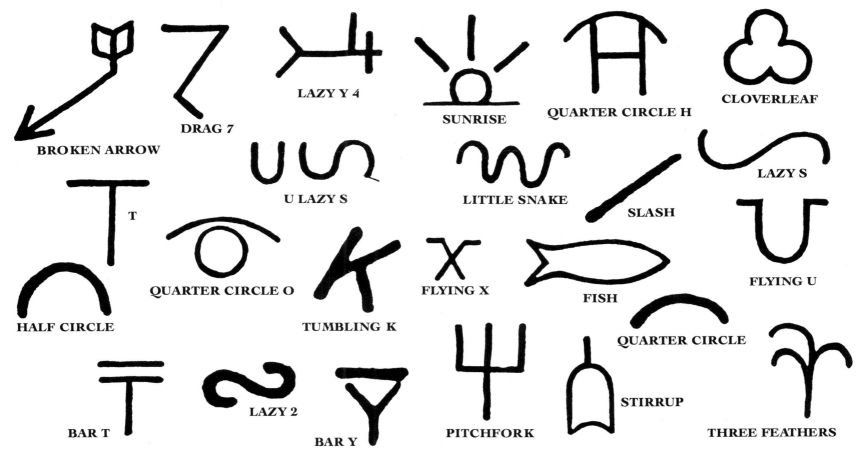

BROKEN ARROW

DRAG 7

LAZY Y 4

SUNRISE

QUARTER CIRCLE H

CLOVERLEAF

U LAZY S

LITTLE SNAKE

LAZY S

SLASH

T

QUARTER CIRCLE O

FLYING X

FISH

FLYING U

HALF CIRCLE

TUMBLING K

QUARTER CIRCLE

BAR T

LAZY 2

BAR Y

PITCHFORK

STIRRUP

THREE FEATHERS

signing a brand, a cattleman was careful to avoid letters and numbers that could be altered by cattle thieves, since a simple stroke of the running iron could change a "3" into an "8" or a "B," a "C" into an "O," and an "I" into a dozen other letters. Legitimate brands were always registered with the county clerk, and any steer caught with an unrecorded brand was liable to be confiscated by the government.

Branding was introduced to North America by Hernando Cortez, who burned an indelible "C" on the cheeks of his Indian slaves and three Christian crosses on the hides of his Andalusian cattle. The Christian cross and two of its variants, the anchor and the swastika, later became the most popular picture brands in the West. The anchor, symbol of hope, tranquillity, and patience, was the emblem of Saint Clement, patron saint of tanners, and it was believed that cattle branded with his sign would surely produce good leather. Belief in the swastika, symbol of the sun and of creation, lapsed in the 1940s, when its adoption by the Third Reich caused many an embarrassed Westerner to switch to another sign.

Directory of Sources

When contacting retailers or manufacturers, please remember that all prices listed in this book are subject to change.

ACCESSORIES

Retailers

CUTTER BILL WESTERN WORLD
5818 LBJ Freeway
Dallas, Texas 75240

H. KAUFFMAN & SONS SADDLERY
139 East 24th Street
New York, New York 10010

NEIMAN-MARCUS
1618 Main Street
Dallas, Texas 75201

RYON SADDLERY
2601 N. Main Street
Fort Worth, Texas 76106

SHEPLERS
P.O. Box 7702
Wichita, Kansas 67277

Manufacturers

BOB BLACKWOOD SPURS & RODEO EQUIPMENT
P.O. Box 351
Farmersville, Texas 75031

CARTIER
16 East 52nd Street
New York, New York 10022

TOM TAYLOR COMPANY
P.O. Box 6
Sandia Park, New Mexico 87407

VOGT WESTERN SILVER LTD.
P.O. Box 2309
Turlock, California 95380

WARNER'S TACK MANUFACTURING CORP.
4414 Ellis Lane
El Monte, California 91734

BELTS

Retailers

RYON SADDLERY
2601 N. Main Street
Fort Worth, Texas 76106

Manufacturers

NOCONA BELT COMPANY
110 W. Willow Street
Nocona, Texas 76255

TOM TAYLOR COMPANY
P.O. Box 6
Sandia Park, New Mexico 87407

TEX TAN WESTERN LEATHER COMPANY
Box 711
Yoakum, Texas 77995

BOOTS

Retailers

H. KAUFFMAN & SONS SADDLERY
139 East 24th Street
New York, New York 10010

RYON SADDLERY
2601 N. Main Street
Fort Worth, Texas 76106

Manufacturers

ACME BOOT COMPANY, INC.
P.O. Box 749
Clarksville, Tennessee 37040

AUSTIN-HALL BOOT COMPANY
Box 12368
El Paso, Texas 79912

DURANGO BOOT COMPANY
P.O. Box 10
Franklin, Tennessee 37064

JOHN A. FRYE SHOE COMPANY, INC.
84 Chestnut Street
Marlboro, Massachusetts 01752

THE JUSTIN COMPANIES
P.O. Box 548
Fort Worth, Texas 76101

TONY LAMA COMPANY, INC.
1137 Tony Lama Street
El Paso, Texas 79915

LUCCHESE BOOTS
1226 East Houston Street
San Antonio, Texas 78205

NOCONA BOOT COMPANY
Box 599
E. Highway 82
Nocona, Texas 76255

TEXAS BOOT COMPANY
Forrest Avenue
Lebanon, Tennessee 37087

WRANGLER BOOTS
P.O. Box 60485
Nashville, Tennessee 37206

BRIDLES AND BITS
Retailers
H. KAUFFMAN & SONS
SADDLERY
139 East 24th Street
New York, New York 10010

RYON SADDLERY
2601 N. Main Street
Fort Worth, Texas 76106

Manufacturers
RENALDE, CROCKETT & KELLY
944 Pearl Street
Boulder, Colorado 80302

SIMCO LEATHER
COMPANY, INC.
1800 Daisy Street
Chattanooga, Tennessee 37406

TOM TAYLOR COMPANY
P.O. Box 6
Sandia Park, New Mexico 87407

TEX TAN WESTERN
LEATHER COMPANY
Box 711
Yoakum, Texas 77995

VOGT WESTERN SILVER LTD.
P.O. Box 2309
Turlock, California 95380

BUCKLES
Retailers
RYON SADDLERY
2601 N. Main Street
Fort Worth, Texas 76106

Manufacturers
BARRY KIESELSTEIN
ENTERPRISES
67 Park Avenue
New York, New York 10016
(correspondence only)

TOM TAYLOR COMPANY
P.O. Box 6
Sandia Park, New Mexico 87407

TEX TAN WESTERN
LEATHER COMPANY
Box 711
Yoakum, Texas 77995

VOGT WESTERN SILVER LTD.
P.O. Box 2309
Turlock, California 95380

CHAPS
Retailers
CUTTER BILL WESTERN
WORLD
5818 LBJ Freeway
Dallas, Texas 75240

RYON SADDLERY
2601 N. Main Street
Fort Worth, Texas 76106

SHEPLERS
P.O. Box 7702
Wichita, Kansas 67277

Manufacturers
BAR W CHAPS
212 N.W. 24th, P.O. Box 4468
Fort Worth, Texas 76106

RODEO SHOP OF
FORT WORTH, INC.
Box 12693
Fort Worth, Texas 76116

ROGUE LEATHER COMPANY
754 S.W. 6th Street
Grants Pass, Oregon 97526

TEX TAN WESTERN
LEATHER COMPANY
Box 711
Yoakum, Texas 77995

HATS
Manufacturers
BAILEY HAT COMPANY
2558 San Fernando Road
Los Angeles, California 90065

RESISTOL HATS
by Byer-Rolnick
601 Marion Drive
Garland, Texas 75040
STETSON HAT COMPANY, INC.
3601 Leonard Road
Saint Joseph, Missouri 64502

JEANS
Retailers
CUTTER BILL WESTERN
WORLD
5818 LBJ Freeway
Dallas, Texas 75240

Manufacturers
LE POCHE. *See* Cutter Bill Western
World

SASSON JEANS, INC.
498 Seventh Avenue
New York, New York 10018

LEVI STRAUSS & COMPANY
2 Embarcadero Center
San Francisco, California 94106

WRANGLER WESTERN WEAR
by Wrangler Menswear
Division of Blue Bell, Inc.
335 Church Street
Greensboro, North Carolina 27402

OUTERWEAR
Retailers

BILLY MARTIN'S
WESTERN WEAR
68th Street and Madison Avenue
New York, New York 10021

Countryside Mall, #731
2601 U S Highway 19 North
Clearwater, Florida 33519

CUTTER BILL WESTERN
WORLD
5818 LBJ Freeway
Dallas, Texas 75240

H. KAUFFMAN & SONS
SADDLERY
139 East 24th Street
New York, New York 10010

NEIMAN-MARCUS
1618 Main Street
Dallas, Texas 75201

SHEPLERS
P.O. Box 7702
Wichita, Kansas 67277

Manufacturers

ALTMAN WESTERN LEATHERS
3005 Elm Street
Dallas, Texas 75226

CHAR DESIGNS, INC.
P.O. Box 427
Tesuque, New Mexico 87574

COMFY by
Raven Industries, Inc.
P.O. Box 1007
Sioux Falls, South Dakota 57101

GERRY WESTERN
6260 Downing Street
Denver, Colorado 80216

H. D. LEE COMPANY, INC.
P.O. Box 2940
Shawnee Mission, Kansas 66201

MAHOPA
Box 202
Laurens, New York 13796

BERT PALEY LTD.
Division of After Six, Inc.
1290 Avenue of the Americas
New York, New York 10019

SCHOTT BROTHERS, INC.
441 High Street
Perth Amboy, New Jersey 08861

SCULLY LEATHERWEAR
725 E. Washington Boulevard
Los Angeles, California 90021

SEDGEFIELD SPORTSWEAR
COMPANY
P.O. Box 76186
Greensboro, North Carolina 27420

TREGO'S WESTWEAR, INC.
2215 Oklahoma Avenue, P.O. Box 927
Woodward, Oklahoma 73801

RODEO EQUIPMENT
Manufacturers

BOB BLACKWOOD SPURS &
RODEO EQUIPMENT
P.O. Box 351
Farmersville, Texas 75031

CAMARILLO ENTERPRISES,
INC.
P.O. Box 155
Clements, California 95227

TEX TAN WESTERN
LEATHER COMPANY
Box 711
Yoakum, Texas 77995

SADDLES
Retailers

H. KAUFFMAN & SONS
SADDLERY
139 East 24th Street
New York, New York 10010

RYON SADDLERY
2601 N. Main Street
Fort Worth, Texas 76106

Manufacturers

BOB BLACKWOOD SPURS &
RODEO EQUIPMENT
P.O. Box 351
Farmersville, Texas 75031

CIRCLE Y, INC.
602 Front Street, P.O. Box 797
Yoakum, Texas 77995

COLORADO SADDLERY
COMPANY
1631 15th Street
Denver, Colorado 80202

PRICE MCLAUCHLIN
SADDLE SHOP
343 N. Saginaw Boulevard
Saginaw, Texas 76179

SIMCO LEATHER
COMPANY, INC.
1800 Daisy Street
Chattanooga, Tennessee 37406

TEX TAN WESTERN
LEATHER COMPANY
Box 711
Yoakum, Texas 77995

SHIRTS
Retailers

CUTTER BILL WESTERN
WORLD
5818 LBJ Freeway
Dallas, Texas 75240

RYON SADDLERY
2601 N. Main Street
Fort Worth, Texas 76106

Manufacturers
CHAMPION WESTERN WEAR
108 South Santa Fe
Denver, Colorado 80223

CHAR DESIGNS, INC.
P.O. Box 427
Tesuque, New Mexico 87574

DICKSON-JENKINS
MANUFACTURING COMPANY

P.O. Box 628
202 St. Louis Avenue
Fort Worth, Texas 76102

HANDLER-FENTON and
FENTON WESTERNS
224 W. Alameda Avenue
Denver, Colorado 80223

H BAR C RANCHWEAR by
Halpern & Christenfeld
101 West 21st Street
New York, New York 10011

KARMAN WESTERN APPAREL
1513 Wazee Street
Denver, Colorado 80202

MILLER WESTERN WEAR
P.O. Box 5407
8500 Zuni Street
Denver, Colorado 80217

THE PRIOR COMPANY
1133 South Platte River Drive
Denver, Colorado 80223

VAN HEUSEN COMPANY
1290 Avenue of the Americas
New York, New York 10019

WRANGLER WESTERN WEAR
by Wrangler Menswear
Division of Blue Bell, Inc.
335 Church Court
Greensboro, North Carolina 27402

SPURS
Retailers

H. KAUFFMAN & SONS
SADDLERY

139 East 24th Street
New York, New York 10010

RYON SADDLERY
2601 N. Main Street
Fort Worth, Texas 76106

Manufacturers
BOB BLACKWOOD SPURS &
RODEO EQUIPMENT
P.O. Box 351
Farmersville, Texas 75031

RENALDE, CROCKETT & KELLY
944 Pearl Street
Boulder, Colorado 80302

SUITS
Retailers
CUTTER BILL WESTERN
WORLD
5818 LBJ Freeway
Dallas, Texas 75240

NUDIE
5015 Lankershim Boulevard
North Hollywood, California 91601

SHEPLERS
P.O. Box 7702
Wichita, Kansas 67277

Manufacturers
ABOVE THE CROWD
c/o Arlene Sportswear
498 Seventh Avenue
New York, New York 10018

AFTER SIX FORMALS
1290 Avenue of the Americas
New York, New York 10019

OLEG CASSINI
1290 Avenue of the Americas
New York, New York 10019

CHAR DESIGNS, INC.
P.O. Box 427
Tesuque, New Mexico 87574

CONDOR
400 West 30th Street
Los Angeles, California 90007

COUNTRY BRITCHES
1290 Avenue of the Americas
New York, New York 10019

H BAR C RANCHWEAR by
Halpern & Christenfeld
101 West 21st Street
New York, New York 10011

LASSO WESTERN WEAR
6623 S. Zarzamora Street
San Antonio, Texas 78221

NIVER WESTERN WEAR, INC.
1221 Hemphill Street
Fort Worth, Texas 76104

SALAMINDER. *See* Cutter Bill
Western World

SCULLY LEATHERWEAR
725 E. Washington Boulevard
Los Angeles, California 90021

TRAILERS
Manufacturers

CHEROKEE MANUFACTURING
COMPANY
Industrial Park Road
Sweetwater, Tennessee 37874

GENERAL TRAILER
CORPORATION
11993 Ravenna Road/Route 44
Chardon, Ohio 44024

188

HARTMAN TRAILER
MANUFACTURING COMPANY, INC.
7 Walnut Street
Perkasie, Pennsylvania 18944

JOHNSTON TRAILERS, INC.
Canal Winchester, Ohio 43110

TRUCKS & JEEPS
Manufacturers

CHEVROLET MOTOR DIVISION
General Motors Corporation
General Motors Building
Detroit, Michigan 48202

DODGE by
Chrysler Corporation
12000 Lynn Townsend Drive
Detroit, Michigan 48288

FORD MOTOR COMPANY
American Road
Dearborn, Michigan 48121

INTERNATIONAL HARVESTER
COMPANY
One Pennsylvania Plaza
New York, New York 10001

JEEP by
American Motors Corporation
27777 Franklin Road
Southfield, Michigan 48034

Index